Mountain Bike Virginia

MOUNTAIN BIKE VIRGINIA

Maps created by Beachway Press
Illustrations by Mike Francis
Photos by Scott Adams
Consulting editor, John Phillips
DCR—Department of Conservation and Recreation

ISBN 1-882997-04-2

Library of Congress Cataloging-in-Publication Data
     Adams, Scott
     Mountain Bike Virginia : An Atlas of Virginia's Greatest Off-Road Bicycle Rides / by Scott Adams. 1st ed. Springfield, VA : Beachway Press, c1995.
     256 pages : Illustrations, Photographs, Maps
        1. All-terrain cycling—Virginia—Guidebooks.
Virginia—Guidebooks.
95-076503
CIP

Published by Beachway Press
9201 Beachway Lane
Springfield, VA 22153-1441

Printed in the United State of America

10 9 8 7 6 5 4 3

Mountain Bike Virginia

An Atlas of Virginia's Greatest Off-Road
Bicycle Rides

by Scott Adams

Beachway Press

Beachway Press' Mountain Bike America Series

Dear Readers:

Every effort was made to make this the most accurate, informative, and easy-to-use guidebook on the planet. Any comments, suggestions, and corrections regarding this guide or any of its rides are welcome and should be sent to:

Beachway Press
c/o editorial dept.
9201 Beachway Lane
Springfield, VA 22153

We'd love to hear from you so we can make future editions and future guides even better.

Thanks and happy trails!

Table of Contents

If you're not part of the solution,
then you're part of the problem.

Introduction

Welcome to the new generation of bicycling! Indeed, the sport has evolved dramatically from the thin-tired, featherweight-frame days of old. The sleek geometry and lightweight frames of racing bicycles, still the heart and soul of bicycling worldwide, have lost much ground in recent years, *unpaving* the way for the mountain bike, which now accounts for the majority of all bicycle sales in the U.S. And with this change comes a new breed of cyclist, less concerned with smooth roads and long rides, who thrives in places once inaccessible to the mortal road bike.

The mountain bike, with its knobby tread and reinforced frame, takes cyclists to places once unheard of—down rugged mountain trails, through streams of rushing water and thick mud, across the frozen Alaskan tundra, and even to work in the city. There seem to be few limits on what this fat-tired beast can do and where it can take us. Few obstacles stand in its way, few boundaries slow its progress. Except for one—its own success. If trail closure means little to you now, read on and discover how a trail can be here today and gone tomorrow. With so many new off-road cyclists taking to the trails each year, its no wonder trail access hinges precariously between universal acceptance and complete termination. But a little work on your part can go a long way to preserving trail access for future use. Nothing is more crucial to the survival of mountain biking itself than to read the examples set forth in the following pages and practice their message. Then turn to the maps, pick out your favorite ride, and hit the dirt!

WHAT THIS BOOK IS ABOUT

Within these pages you will find everything you need to know about off-road bicycling in the state of Virginia. This guidebook begins by exploring the fascinating history of the mountain bike itself, then goes on to discuss everything from the health benefits of off-road cycling to tips and techniques for bicycling over logs and up hills. Also included are the types of clothing to keep you comfortable and in style, essential equipment ideas to keep your rides smooth and trouble-free, and descriptions of off-road terrain to prepare you for the kinds of bumps and bounces you can expect to encounter. The two major provisions of this book, though, are its unique and detailed maps and relentless dedication to trail preservation.

Each of the 30 rides included in this book is accompanied by four very different maps. A **location map** shows where each ride is in relation to the rest of Virginia; the **3D profile map** displays an accurate view of the each ride's ups and downs in three dimensions, the **road map** leads you through each ride and is accompanied by detailed directions, and a **3D surface area map** provides a fascinating view of the surrounding topography and landscape.

Without open trails, the maps in this book are virtually useless. Cyclists must learn to be responsible for the trails they use and to share these trails with others. This guide book addresses such issues as why trail use has become so controversial, what can be done to improve the image of mountain biking, how to have fun and ride responsibly, on-the-spot trail repair techniques, trail maintenance hotlines for each trail, and the worldwide-standard *Rules of the Trail*.

Each of the 30 rides is complete with maps, trail descriptions and directions, local history, and a quick-reference information board including such items as trail-maintenance hotlines, park schedules, costs, and alternative maps.

It's important to note that mountain bike rides tend to take longer than road rides because the average speed is often much slower. Average speeds can vary from a climbing pace of three to four miles per hour to 12 to 13 miles per hour on flatter roads and trails. Keep this in mind when planning your trip.

MOUNTAIN BIKE BEGINNINGS

It seems the mountain bike, originally designed for lunatic adventurists bored with straight lines, clean clothes, and smooth tires, has become globally popular in as short a time as it would take to race down a mountain trail.

Like many things of a revolutionary nature, the mountain bike was born on the west coast. But unlike roller blades, purple hair, and the peace sign, the concept of the off-road bike cannot be credited solely to the imaginative Californians—they were just the first to make waves.

The design of the first off-road specific bike was based on the geometry of the old Schwinn Excelsior, a one-speed, camel-back cruiser with balloon tires. Joe Breeze was the creator behind it, and in 1977 he built 10 of these "Breezers" for himself and his Marin County, California, friends at $750 apiece—a bargain.

Breeze was a serious competitor in bicycle racing, placing 13th in the 1977 U.S. Road Racing National Championships. After races, he and friends would scour local bike shops hoping to find old bikes they could then restore.

It was the 1941 Schwinn Excelsior, for which Breeze paid just five dollars, that began to shape and change bicycling history forever. After taking the bike home, removing the fenders, oiling the chain, and pumping up the tires, Breeze hit the dirt. He loved it.

His inspiration, while forerunning, was not altogether unique. On the opposite end of the country, nearly 2,500 miles from Marin County, east coast bike bums were also growing restless. More and more old, beat-up clunkers were being restored and modified. These behemoths often weighed as much as 80 pounds and were so reinforced they seemed virtually indestructible. But rides that take just 40 minutes on today's 25-pound featherweights took the steel-toed-boot- and blue-jean-clad bikers of the late 1970s and early 1980s nearly four hours to complete.

Not until 1981 was it possible to purchase a production mountain bike, but local retailers found these ungainly bicycles difficult to sell and rarely kept them in stock. By 1983, however, mountain bikes were no longer such a fringe item, and large bike manufacturers quickly jumped into the action, producing their own versions of the off-road bike. By the 1990s, the mountain bike had firmly established its place with bicyclists of nearly all ages and abilities, and now command, nearly 90 percent of the U.S. bike market.

There are many reasons for the mountain bike's success in becoming the hottest two-wheeled vehicle in the nation. They are much friendlier to the cyclist than traditional road bikes because of their comfortable upright position and shock-absorbing fat tires. And because of the health-conscious, environmentalist movement of the late 1980s and 1990s, people are more activity minded and seek nature on a closer front than paved roads can allow. The mountain bike gives you these things and takes you far away from the daily grind—even if you're only minutes from the city.

MOUNTAIN BIKING INTO SHAPE

If your objective is to get in shape and lose weight, then you're on the right track, because mountain biking is one of the best ways to get started.

One way many of us have lost weight in this sport is the crash-and-burn-it-off method. Picture this: you're speeding uncontrollably down a vertical drop that you realize you shouldn't be on—only after it is too late. Your front wheel lodges into a rut and launches you through endless weeds, trees, and pointy rocks before coming to an abrupt halt in a puddle of thick mud. Surveying the damage, you discover, with the layers of skin, body parts, and lost confidence littering the trail above, that those unwanted pounds have been shed—permanently. Instant weight loss.

There is, of course, a more conventional (and quite a bit less painful) approach to losing weight and gaining fitness on a mountain bike. It's called the workout, and bicycles provide an ideal way to get physical. Take a look at some of the benefits associated with cycling.

Cycling helps you shed pounds without gimmicky diet fads or

The Maps

I don't want anyone, by any means, to feel restricted to just these roads and trails that I have mapped. I hope you will have the same adventurous spirit and use these maps as a platform to dive into Virginia's backcountry, discovering new routes for yourself. One of the best ways to begin this is to simply turn the map upside down and ride the course in reverse. The change in perspective is fantastic and the ride should feel quite different. With this in mind, it will be like getting two distinctly different rides on each map.

For your own purposes, you may wish to copy the directions for the course onto a small sheet to help you while riding, or photocopy the map and cue sheet to take with you. These pages can be carried with you easily using the BarMap© or BarMap OTG© (note description on last page), or can simply be folded into a bike bag or stuffed into a jersey pocket. Please remember to slow or even stop when you want to read the map.

After a short introduction, there is a profile map of each route followed by a cue sheet, which provides detailed directions and information about each ride.

Map Legend

(81) Interstate Road	★ Start of Ride
(522) U.S. Highway Road	⌒→ Directional Arrows
(654) State Road	● Easy
Maintained Dirt Road	▫ Moderate
Unmaintained Jeep Trail	◆ Difficult
Singletrack Trail	◆◆ Most Difficult
Highlighted Route	☼ Overlook
Ntl. Forest/County Boundaries	▲ Campground
State Boundaries	𝄴 Hiking-Only Trails
Railroad Tracks	▶ Shelter
Power Lines	ǀ Gate
Appalachian Trail	⚞ Ski Resort
Rivers or Streams	△ Radio Tower

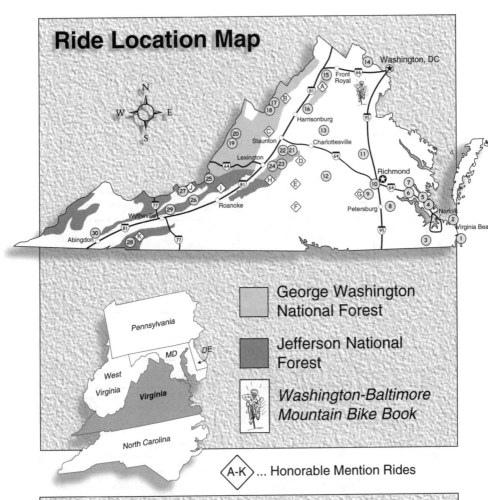

Ride Location Map

George Washington National Forest

Jefferson National Forest

Washington-Baltimore Mountain Bike Book

A-K ... Honorable Mention Rides

1. Back Bay to False Cape
2. Seashore State Park
3. Great Dismal Swamp
4. Harwoods Mill
5. Newport News Park
6. Waller Mill Park
7. York River State Park
8. Petersburg National Battlefield
9. Pocahontas State Park
10. Belle Isle
11. Poor Farm Park
12. Cumberland State Forest
13. Charlottesville Dirt Ride
14. Great Falls National Park
15. Elizabeth Furnace
16. Massanutten Mountain
17. Reddish Knob
18. Flagpole
19. Ellis Loop Trail
20. Hidden Valley
21. Sherando Lake Loop
22. Big Levels
23. Henry Lanum Trail
24. Blue Ridge Dirt Ride
25. Potts Mountain
26. Brush Mountain
27. Mountain Lake
28. Mount Rogers Loop
29. New River Trail State Park
30. Virginia Creeper Trail

Courses at a Glance

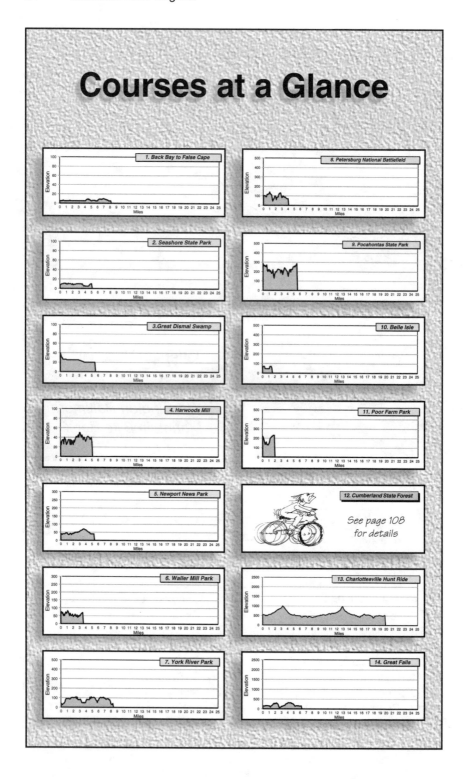

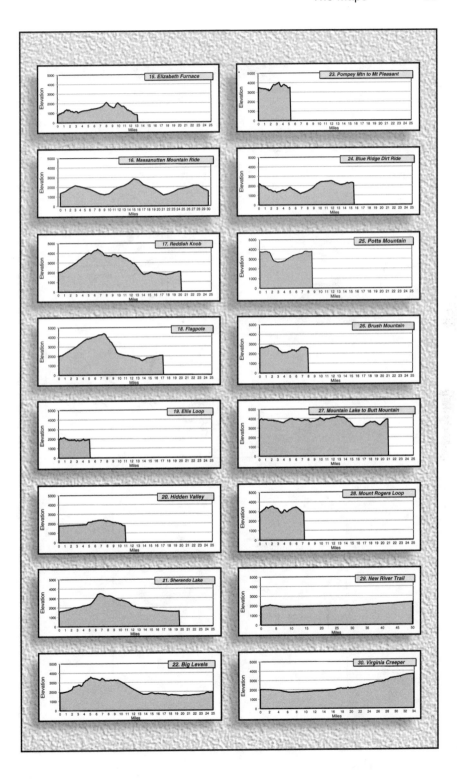

How To Use These Maps

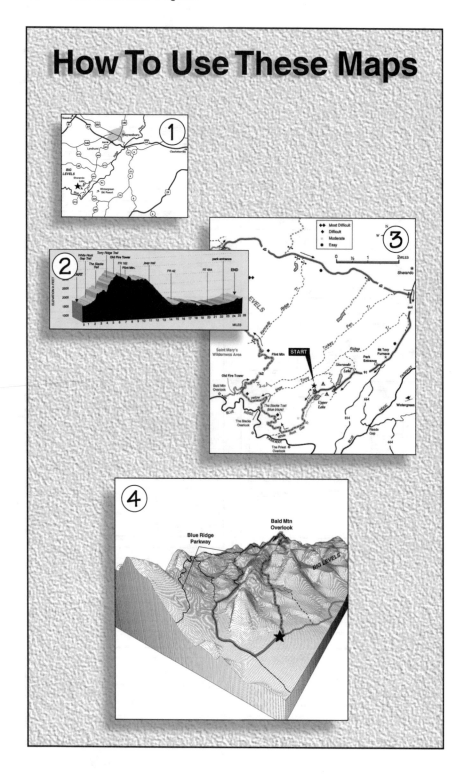

(1) **Location Map.** This map helps you find your way to the start of each ride from the nearest sizeable town or city. Coupled with the detailed directions at the beginning of the cue, this map should visually lead you to where you need to be to hit the trails.

(2) **3D Profile Map.** This three-dimensional profile gives you a cross-sectional look at the ride's ups and downs. Elevation is labeled on the left, mileage is indicated on the bottom, towns and points of interest are shown above the map in **bold**. Road and trail names, also shown above the map, are labeled in *italics*.

(3) **Road Map.** This is your primary guide to each ride. It shows all of the accessible roads and trails, points of interest, water, towns, landmarks, and geographical features. It also distinguishes trails from roads and paved roads from unpaved roads. The selected route is highlighted, and directional arrows point the way.

(4) **3D Surface Area Map.** This three-dimensional look at the earth's surface within the area of the selected ride gives you an accurate representation of the surrounding topography and landscape. The map has been rotated for the best view and includes important roads and trails as well as distinguishable features for points of reference.

Ride Information Board *(at the end of each ride section)*. This is a small bulletin board with important information concerning each ride.

- The **Trail Maintenance Hotline** is the direct number for the local land managers in charge of all the trails within the selected ride. Use this hotline right away if there is ever a problem with trail erosion, damage, or misuse.
- **Cost.** What money, if any, you may need to carry with you for park entrance fees or tolls.
- **Schedule.** This tells you what time trails open and close, if on private or park land.
- **Maps.** This is a list of other maps to supplement the maps in this book. They are listed in order from most detailed to most general.

1. Back Bay to False Cape

Start: *Back Bay Visitors Center* **Terrain:** *Dirt roads, sandy trails, beach*
Length: *27.7 miles total*   **Riding Time:** *1 – 4 hours*
Rating: *Easy*   **Other Uses:** *Hiking, camping*

Dunes at False Cape.

Flase Cape State Park, located on the southeastern tip of Virginia, is the least-visited park in the state of Virginia, averaging fewer than 22,000 visitors annually. However, False Cape isn't for everyone.

To get there, one must be willing to travel off-road by bicycle, foot, or boat at least 10 miles round-trip through the nearly 8,000 acres of Back Bay National Wildlife Refuge. There is no vehicular access to the park, and hardy adventurers must lug in their own water, food, shelter, and hefty cans of bug spray (False Cape is renowned for its large insect population).

The reward is one of the most isolated and unspoiled coastal environments on the East Coast.

Annually, hundreds of species of birds, including snow and Canadian geese, tundra swans, and ducks, make this thin strip of Atlantic coastline their fall and winter home. River otters, white-tailed deer, mink, muskrats, opossums, and raccoons also share this coastal habitat with a few of the non-native species such as False Cape's wild horses and feral pigs.

Wild dunes and forests of loblolly pine, maple, and gnarled live oak grow right up to the persistent Atlantic surf, where sandpipers dodge the crashing waves and forage for meals in the sand. Farther out in the ocean, brown pelicans and osprey dive into the ocean in search of fish.

The adventure begins at Back Bay's visitor contact station, just south of the tiny coastal community of Sandbridge. Parking is plentiful, and the station is equipped with restrooms, telephone, maps, and information about the area. And since no motorized vehicles are allowed past this point, there is no other logical alternative but to leave the car and unpack your bike.

The bike route starts on the east side of the visitor contact station and follows either the east or west dike south toward False Cape. Both dikes are topped with gravel and are well suited for cycling. Immediately before the Dune Trail, the two dikes split, but reconnect at each of the three cross dikes on your way south.

The arrangement of the different dikes and cross dikes throughout the Back Bay Refuge form large areas of marsh and wetland into what is called an impoundment. Three of these impoundments, or pools, exist in Back Bay, all of which are drained in the summer months. In fall and winter, the impoundments are filled, then planted with grass, plants, and other vegetation necessary as sustenance for the wintering birds and waterfowl this refuge serves to protect. Both the east and west dikes lead directly into False Cape State Park, so choose either one for the journey through Back Bay.

Cyclists may also choose to ride the five-mile route along the beach. Be aware, though, that the best time is at low tide when there's plenty of hard, wet sand on which to ride. If you want to come back along the beach, be sure to keep an eye on the incoming tide.

Once you reach False Cape State Park you may find its coastal habitat very similar to Back Bay's—beautiful and unspoiled. There are numerous sights along the many miles of the park's bicycle routes, including the Wash Woods cemetery and church site, and False Cape's wildlife lookout tower—a perfect place to view tundra swans and snow geese.

At some point in the nineteenth century, a small community called Wash Woods developed on what is now the state park. Most of its residents were farmers and fishermen who carried their small parcels of crops and fish across Back Bay by boat to sell on the mainland. However, amid heavy storms and a battering ocean, and the fatal blow of a massive hurricane

(continued on page 43)

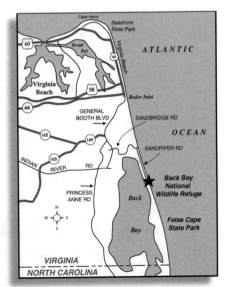

Back Bay to False Cape

☞   From Virginia Beach – Travel **east** on Shore Drive (U.S. 60) until it turns right and becomes **Atlantic Avenue**. At **40th Street** get in the **right-hand lane**. This is **Pacific Avenue**. Pacific Avenue becomes **General Booth Blvd** after crossing **Rudee Inlet Bridge**. Go 7 miles on **General Booth Blvd**, then turn **left** on **Princess Anne Road**. Go 0.5 miles to the **first light** and turn **left** on **Sandbridge Road**. Take **Sandbridge Road** 5.6 miles, then turn **right** on **Sandpiper Road**. Follow **Sandpiper Road** along the ocean to **Back Bay National Wildlife Refuge**.

MILES   DIRECTIONS

0.0   **START** at the **Back Bay National Wildlife Refuge Visitor Contact Station**. The bike trail starts on the east side of the visitors center. Travel **south** along Back Bay's **INTERIOR DIKE** toward False Cape State Park.

0.2   The **INTERIOR DIKE** splits into east and west dikes just before the Dune Trail Boardwalk. Cross-dikes connect the east and west dikes three separate times before the False Cape State Park line. Take either the **EAST DIKE** or **WEST DIKE** to False Cape.

0.6   Begin passing **Pool C**, a large impoundment of marsh and wetland used to accommodate wintering birds and waterfowl. This and the other two impoundments are drained during the summer.

2.0   Reach the **first cross-dike**. Continue south on either the

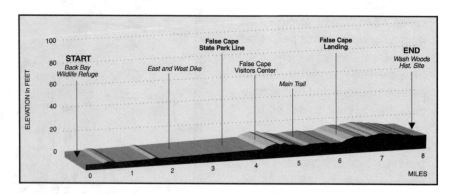

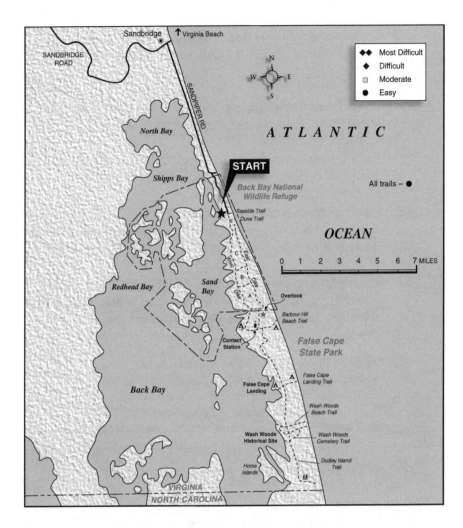

EAST or WEST DIKE. Begin passing **Pool B.**

2.5 Reach the **second cross-dike.** Continue south on either the **East** or **West Dike.** Begin passing **Pool A.**

3.3 Reach the **third cross-dike** and **False Cape State Park.** Regardless of which dike you were riding on, you will enter False Cape on the **BARBOUR HILL INTERPRETIVE TRAIL,** which forms a 2.4-mile loop. This interpretive nature trail passes the **state park contact station** and the **observation tower (overlook).** The observation tower is great for viewing the island's unique wildlife in its natural environment.

4.25   From the **Barbour Hill Beach Trail** and the **Visitors Contact Station**, follow the MAIN TRAIL south toward False Cape Landing.

6.3   Reach **False Cape Landing Trail**. Continue straight on the MAIN TRAIL toward Wash Woods Historical Site.

7.5   Pass the **Wash Woods Beach Trail** (0.8 miles east to the Atlantic). Continue **straight** on the MAIN TRAIL.

7.8   Pass the **Wash Woods Interpretive Trail** (0.7 miles east to the Atlantic/0.1 miles west to the Wash Woods Environmental Education Center). Continue **straight** on the MAIN TRAIL.

8.1   Turn **right** on the WASH WOODS CEMETERY TRAIL. Almost immediately you will arrive at the old town of **Wash Woods' cemetery and church site**. *Bicycles are not permitted beyond this point.*

       5 miles – Back Bay to False Cape along the beach.
       4 miles – False Cape to North Carolina along the beach.
       7.5 miles of rideable trails in Back Bay.
       11.2 miles of rideable trails in False Cape.
       27.7 miles – Total trails and beach open to bicycling.

Ride Information

Trail Maintenance Hotline:

    Back Bay National Wildlife Refuge   *(804) 721-2412*
    False Cape State Park   *(804) 426-7128*

Cost:

    $2.00 – Single visit permit (foot/bike)
    Under age 16 – Free

Schedule:

    Back Bay dikes closed from Nov.1 to April 30.
    Beach to False Cape open year-round

Maps:

    USGS maps: Knotts Island, VA, NC; North Bay, VA
    ADC map: Tidewater road map
    Back Bay National Wildlife Refuge trail map
    False Cape State Park trail map

Park signs lead you through this challenging route.

and down the hills alongside the reservoir.

After finishing this section, you are rewarded with a leisurely ride along a forest road before heading toward the *Expert* trail. Don't be fooled by this rating, though. At no time will you plummet down vertical drops to an unknown fate or climb deadly walls of slippery rock! The *Expert* trail in Harwoods Mill was designed to challenge bike handling skills on flat terrain, and for this purpose, it is well suited. Tight corners, quick hills, obstacles, and pure singletrack make this a fun and challenging section of the Harwoods Mill Mountain Bike Trail.

The rest of this roller coaster-like ride leads back to the start by way of dirt forest roads. (Note the clear-cutting in the forested area surrounding you. Let's hope they spare the land around these trails.) As you follow the dirt roads toward Harwoods Mill Park, you will pass many of the trailheads for this mountain bike

(continued on page 61)

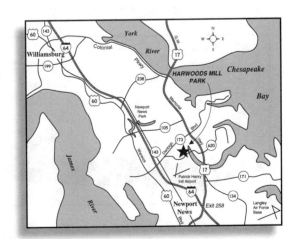

Harwoods Mill

☞   From Newport News – Take I-64 to **Exit-258 north** on U.S. 17 (**George Washington Memorial Highway**). Follow **U.S. 17 north** for about 4 miles, then turn **left** on **Oriana Road (Route 620)**. Cross over Harwoods Mill Reservoir and immediately turn **left** into the parking area for **Harwoods Mill Park**. The mountain bike trail starts across Route 620 from the parking area.

MILES   DIRECTIONS

0.0   **START** at **Harwoods Mill Park** on Old Denbigh Boulevard (Route 620). Cross Old Denbigh Boulevard to the **Harwoods Mill Mountain Bike Trail**. This is marked by a large sign at the start, detailing the rules of the trail. The first section of this trail is labeled **NOVICE,** and is mostly easy terrain. It is marked with a **white band** on wooden trailposts.

0.55   Turn **right** on the DIRT ROAD, heading north.

0.6   Turn **right**, back into the woods, continuing to follow the **NOVICE** singletrack trail.

0.7   Turn **left** on the GRAVEL ROAD that runs parallel with the power lines. Harwoods Mill Reservoir is down the road on the right.

0.8   Turn **right** at the **ADVANCED** trail sign, crossing beneath the power lines. This section is marked with **two yellow bands** and becomes much more difficult.

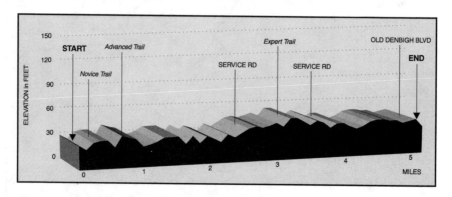

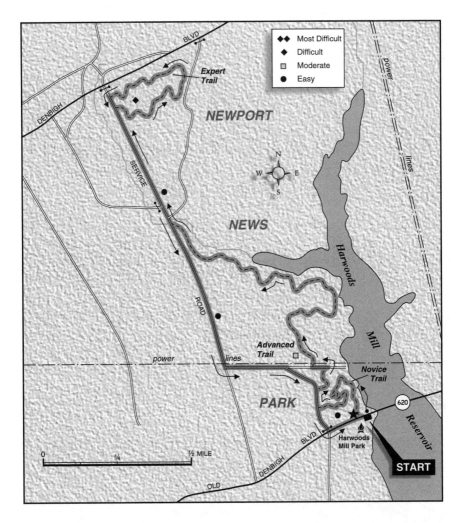

2.2   Leave the *advanced* trail and turn **right** on the **DIRT SERVICE ROAD**. There is a sign at this point directing you 0.4 miles down the road toward the *expert* trail.

2.6   Turn **right** into the woods on the *EXPERT* trail **(three orange bands)**. The *Expert* trail is neither hilly nor steep, but is very technical with obstacles laid across the trail at almost every turn.

3.4   Leave the *expert* trail and turn **left** on the **DIRT SERVICE ROAD**.

4.4   Turn **left** on the **GRAVEL ROAD** that runs parallel to the power lines.

4.6   Turn **right** on the **DIRT ROAD**, heading toward Old Denbigh Boulevard (Route 620).

4.9   Turn **left** on **OLD DENBIGH BOULEVARD (ROUTE 620)**. There is a dirt path on the other side of Old Denbigh Boulevard. Ride along this back to Harwoods Mill Park.

5.2   Reach **Harwoods Mill Park**. If you liked this mountain bike trail system, you'll love the Dogwood Trail up in Waller Mill Park, north of Williamsburg. Dogwood Trail was designed by mountain bikers to accommodate the growing number of off-road cyclists in the region. Its four miles of winding, hilly singletrack may challenge even the best cyclists and trails are open seven days a week.

Ride Information

Trail Maintenance Hotline:

Newport News Park	(804) 888-3333
Eastern VA Mtn. Bike Assoc.	(804) 722-4609

Schedule:

Open daylight to dark all year-round

Maps:

USGS maps:	Poquoson West, VA
ADC map:	Virginia Peninsula road map

(continued from page 57)

park. Jump back on the trails if you wish, but remember, it's a one-way route only. And don't forget to thank the Eastern Virginia Mountain Bike Association and Newport News Department of Parks and Recreation for this fabulous off-road mountain bike trail system.

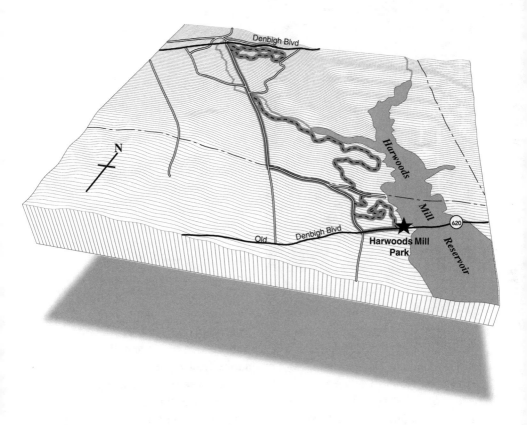

5. Newport News Park

Start: *Info/Campsite Office*   **Terrain:** *Dirt roads*
Length: *5.2 miles*   **Riding Time:** *½ hour – 45 minutes*
Rating: *Easy*   **Other Uses:** *Walking, Jogging*

Yorktown Victory Monument.

The city of Newport News Parks and Recreation Department has done much for its steadily growing number of local mountain bikers, culminating in some great off-road trails and tours for off-road cyclists all along the Virginia Peninsula. One such example is Newport News Park. As one of the nation's largest municipal parks, it has plenty of potential for supporting bicycling, both on and off road.

This leisurely ride through Newport News Park features an easy, off-road loop in the peaceful setting of a wooded environment. The previous chapter discusses the challenges of winding singletrack trails along the Harwoods Mill Mountain Bike Trail in the southern portion of Newport News Park. Both rides, however different, are perfect examples of what Newport News—one of America's oldest cities—has done for mountain biking—one of America's newest sports.

Founded in 1619, Newport News has since become a major American seaport. Early on, though, this point on the Virginia Peninsula at the head of Hampton Roads was no more than the setting for a small English colony trying to establish itself in the "New World."

The city's name derives from the English sea captain Christopher

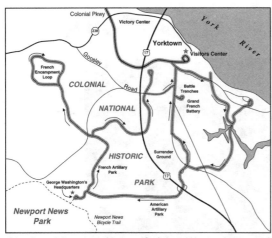

Bike through history at Yorktown's Colonial National Historical Park, accessible from Newport News Park's bicycle trail.

Newport, who sailed from London in 1606 with an expedition of 100 men to settle and explore the New World. Newport and the renowned Captain John Smith landed at what would be named Jamestown on May 14, 1607—the first English colony in America. Plymouth, in Massachusetts, was the first English colony of families in the New World.

Captain Newport sailed back and forth from Jamestown to England over the years for both supplies and news from the homeland. Legend holds that when word spread Captain Newport was sailing back to the colonies, people would rush to the end of the peninsula to hear any news Newport brought back from their homes in England. In 1619, colonists on the peninsula officially adopted the name Newportes Newes for their small town in Virginia.

Since Captain Newport's first landing at Jamestown, events on the Virginia Peninsula continued to shape America's destiny. In October 1781, rebel armies, under the command of General George Washington, battled with muskets and cannons to victory over the Redcoats on the fields at Yorktown. The Revolution—and American Independence—were won from the British.

This independence, however, would not come without a price, and America would soon be at war once again—this time with itself. The land within the boundaries of today's Newport News Park once again soaked in the blood of American soldiers, only now it was brother

(continued on page 66)

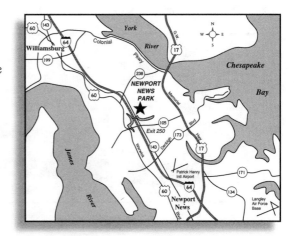

Newport News Park

☞   From Newport News – Take I-64 to **Exit-250** on **Fort Eustis Boulevard (Route 105)** heading **east**. Immediately turn **left** on **Jefferson Avenue (Route 143)** and cross over the City Reservoir. Go approximately one mile to Newport News Park's **second entrance**. Parking, toilets, information, telephones, and bike rentals available.

MILES   DIRECTIONS

0.0   **START** at the **Campsite Office and Information Center**. If you forgot your bike, you can rent one from the Information Center. Turn **right** on the **PARK ACCESS ROAD**, following the "Bike Way" signs toward "Group Sites 1 & 2."

0.2   Pass Dumping Station on the left. Bathrooms available.

0.5   At "Group Site 2," bear **left**, following the "Bike Way" sign

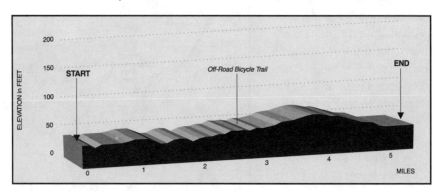

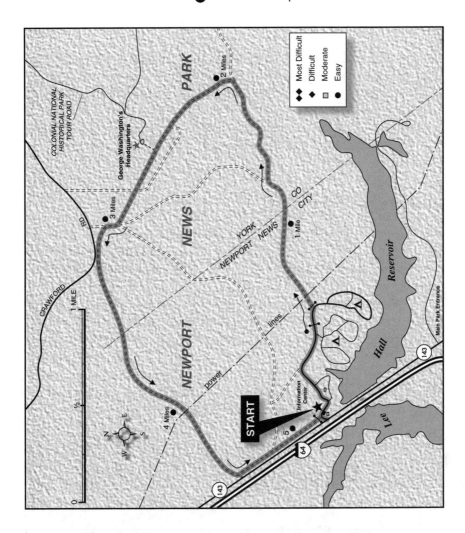

through the gate.

0.6   Turn **left** on the **NEWPORT NEWS PARK "BIKE WAY" (flat, hard-packed dirt road)**. Go around the gate.

2.4   Pass the dirt path on the right leading to **George Washington's Headquarters**.

4.6   Bear **left** at the gate, continuing on the **"BIKE WAY."** This last section runs parallel to Route 143.

5.3   Reach the parking lot.

(continued from page 63)

against brother. On April 16, 1862, the violent thunder of Confederate and Union artillery echoed across the land in what was the first major Civil War engagement on the Peninsula. The Battle of Dam No.1, as it was called, cost both sides over 3,000 men, who were killed, wounded, or missing. After this battle, both sides continued up the Peninsula toward Richmond, where they would meet again to clash in the Seven Days Battle at Richmond.

Today, original Civil War fortifications covering over 10 miles still exist within the park, and most of these 130-year-old fortifications are in excellent condition. Some of the earthworks reach as high as 20 feet. The original Dam No.1 is now beneath the surface of the Lee Hall Reservoir, but can be seen from the footbridge, which crosses over the reservoir.

For cyclists interested in an incredible journey through American history, this easy off-road ride is the perfect way to get started. It begins from the second entrance to Newport News Park, at the Campsite Office entrance on the west side of the Lee Hall Reservoir. There is an information office with restrooms, parking, free literature, and bike rentals, should you leave yours behind. This loop is composed entirely of flat, gravel, and dirt roads that travel five miles through the park's

Ride Information

Trail Maintenance Hotline:

Newport News Park	(804) 886-7912
Colonial National Historical Park	(804) 898-3400

Schedule:

Open daylight to dark all year-round

Maps:

USGS maps:	Yorktown, VA
ADC map:	Virginia Peninsula road map
Newport News Park trail map	

northern section. "Bike way" signs will direct you along the way.

Halfway around this hard-packed dirt loop, you can take a short trail through the woods directly to George Washington's Headquarters, where Washington planned his battle on the eve of victory over the British at Yorktown.

Consider taking the time to travel the nearly 14 miles of paved tour roads through Yorktown's Colonial National Historical Park. These quiet tour roads roll gently through the famous park, allowing for a close-up view of the battlefield on which American forces defeated the great British Army in 1781 and ended British rule over the colonies. Interpretive signs and historical

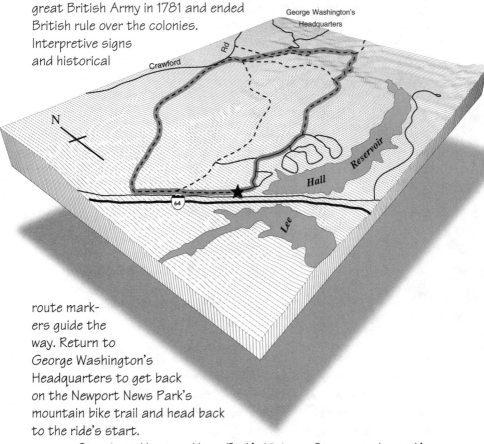

George Washington's
Headquarters

Crawford

Rd

N

Reservoir

Hall

64

Lee

route mark-
ers guide the
way. Return to
George Washington's
Headquarters to get back
on the Newport News Park's
mountain bike trail and head back
to the ride's start.

Stop in at Newport News Park's Visitors Center at the park's main entrance and find out more about the many different paved bike routes the park service has to offer. Most of these routes are selected for their historic, scenic, and recreational interests, and include loops from Yorktown to Jamestown to Williamsburg along gently rolling landscapes and lightly traveled roads.

6. Waller Mill Park

Start: *Trailhead@park entrance*	**Terrain:** *Hilly, wooded singletrack trails*
Length: *4.1 miles*	**Riding Time:** *1 hour*
Rating: *Difficult*	**Other Uses:** *Hiking*

The colony of Jamestown was established in 1607 under sponsorship by the Virginia Company of London. Hoping to make a profit on the land's untapped resources, the Virginia Company embarked on its mission from England in December 1606. Four months later, the first English colonists reached the shores of the New World.

Enjoying the challenges of Dogwood Trail's exciting singletrack.

They landed along the Virginia coast, selecting a safe site with deep water to moor their ships. On May 14, 1607, the colonists began creating what would become the first permanent English settlement in the New World, marking the beginnings of our nation.

Tobacco, the largest cash crop of its time, took root around 1613, stimulating the rapid growth of Jamestown along the James River and other English colonies settling in eastern Virginia. By 1699 the seat of government in Virginia moved to Williamsburg. It remained there until 1780, when Virginians relocated it to Richmond to escape British troops. In 1694, a small college teaching arts and sciences, education, and law was granted its coat of arms— William and Mary is now one of the nation's oldest public colleges.

As towns and cities grew, Britain began imposing greater restrictions and higher taxes on colonists. This oppression ultimately lead to the call for independence. More than six years

Jamestown Settlement

At the Jamestown Settlement near Williamsburg, full-sized replicas of the **Susan Constant**, **Godspeed**, and **Discovery** are docked. These three small ships brought the original colonists to Jamestown in 1607.

after the war against Britain began, America won its independence on the fields of Yorktown, only a few miles from the site of the original settlement. A nation was born and a revolution won on this small piece of historic land along the Virginia Peninsula.

Today, U.S. history is revisited at the Jamestown Settlement, Colonial Williamsburg, and Yorktown Victory Center's living history museums. Within minutes of each other along the Colonial Highway, these museums bring to life the first chapters of America's history.

Moving forward through history to the present day, a new revolution is taking place on Virginia's historic peninsula—mountain biking, of course! In

(continued on page 72)

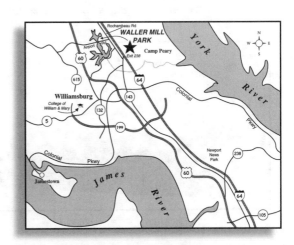

Waller Mill Park

☞   **From Williamsburg** – Take **Richmond Road (U.S. 60) east** approximately 2 miles to **Airport Road**. Turn **right** on **Airport Road (Route 645)**. Go approximately 1½ miles on Airport Road to **Waller Mill Park** entrance on the right. Dogwood Trail begins opposite the entrance to the park.

☞   **From Richmond or Newport News** – Take **I-64** to the **Camp Peary exit**. Make a **hard right** on **Rochambeau Drive**. Go approximately 1½ miles past Bruton High School to **Airport Road**. Turn **left** on **Airport Road (Route 645)**. **Waller Mill Park** entrance is on the left. Dogwood Trail begins opposite the entrance to the park.

MILES   DIRECTIONS

0.0   **START** from the parking lot at **Waller Mill Park**. Follow the entrance road back to the park entrance. Dogwood Trail begins across Airport Road (be careful crossing this road). Immediately across the road and in the woods, Dogwood Trail splits either left or right. Turn **right**, following **DOGWOOD TRAIL** in a **counterclockwise** direction.

(Note: Much like the Harwoods Mill Mountain Bike Trail in Newport News Park, Dogwood Trail must be traveled **one way only—counterclockwise**. While there are no signs dictating one direction over the other, counterclockwise appears to be understood as the preferred direction. The trails twist and turn frequently, the singletrack is very narrow, and passing anywhere on the trail would be difficult and dangerous. Ride

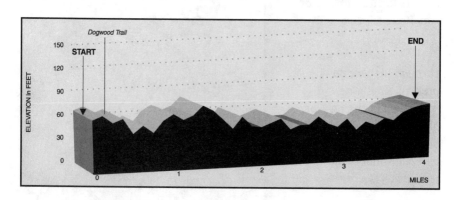

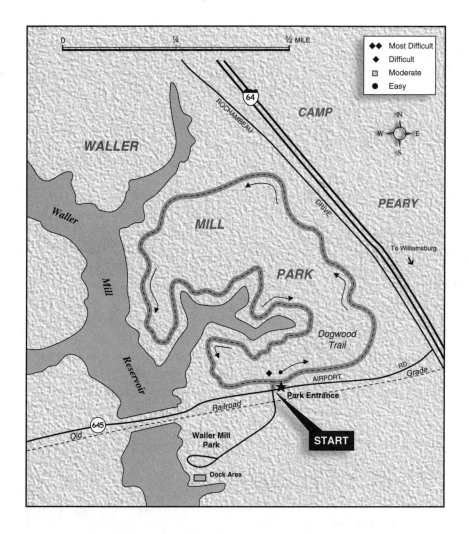

with the flow to avoid any preventable accidents.)

2.3 Pass a wooden bench overlooking the reservoir. This is a perfect spot for a nice break.

3.0 Dogwood Trail contours the hills around the tip of the alcove.

3.5 Head away from the reservoir toward the start of the ride.

Reach the end of the loop at the trailhead for the Dogwood Trail. Care to make another loop before heading home?

(continued from page 69)

addition to Colonial Williamsburg, the Jamestown Settlement, Yorktown Victory Center, Busch Gardens Theme Park, and the College of William and Mary, the Virginia Peninsula has some superior singletrack to offer.

Only minutes from Colonial Williamsburg and a short bike ride from the College of William and Mary, the sensational Dogwood Trail awaits off-road riders. Loaded with hills, singletrack, and inspiring scenery, this four-mile loop contains the most exciting off-road trails in the Tidewater region.

Its home is Waller Mill Park, just off I-64 and cycling distance from Williamsburg. Dogwood Trail is maintained by the city of Williamsburg and is the park's only trail designated for bicycles, so it's particularly important to stay off the park's other trails.

The trail begins across from the park entrance on Airport Road. The first section of Dogwood Trail, traveled counterclockwise, is relatively new. Much of this portion of the trail was cut with the help of the Eastern Virginia Mountain Bike Association and is marked with yellow and orange ribbons. Negotiating many of the dips and turns of this wooded singletrack will get fairly tricky as it cuts through the western half of Waller Mill Park. As the trail nears the reservoir, the terrain rolls more sharply, giving this already challenging trail an increased level of difficulty. At times the trail crests some of the park's small ridges to

Ride Information

Trail Maintenance Hotline:

Waller Mill Park Office	*(804) 220-6178*
Eastern VA Mtn. Bike Association	*(804) 722-4609*

Schedule:

Open 7:00 A.M. – 5:00 P.M. Closed December – March.

Maps:

USGS maps:	*Williamsburg, VA*
ADC map:	*Virginia Peninsula road map*
Waller Mill Park trail map	

reveal scenic views of the reservoir below. Following the loop brings you back to the start of the ride, where you can decide to call it quits or continue for another loop around the Dogwood Trail.

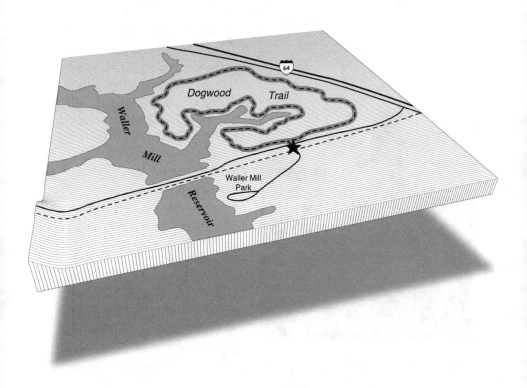

7. York River State Park

Start: *Visitors Center*	**Terrain:** *Singletrack trails, dirt paths*
Length: *8.3 miles*	**Riding Time:** *1 – 1½ hours*
Rating: *Easy*	**Other Uses:** *Hiking, Horseback*

Another great place for off-road cycling in the Tidewater region is York River State Park, located near Williamsburg. Though the terrain is less difficult than the terrain at Waller Mill Park or Harwoods Mill Mountain Bike Trail in Newport News, the more than 15 miles of hiking and bicycling trails in York River State Park offer plenty of enjoyable off-road adventures for nearly all cyclists.

York River State Park is known for its unique environment. Fresh water from the Pamunkey and Mattaponi (mat-a-pone-EYE) Rivers converges approximately 10 miles upriver to form the York River, which then mixes with the salt water of the Chesapeake. The result of this convergence of fresh and salt water creates a habitat rich in marine and plant life.

At some point in history, long ago, the ocean covered nearly all of Tidewater Virginia up to Richmond. The Eastern Shore, Chesapeake Bay, Virginia Beach, and most of Eastern Virginia up to the city of Richmond lay underneath hundreds of feet of ocean water. Today, fossil remains of prehistoric shellfish, sharks, and even whales can be found along the banks of the York River and its tributary streams near the park.

In the 17th and 18th centuries, when tobacco was the cash crop of the commonwealth, York River State Park was actually the site of a public tobacco warehouse called Taskinas

If you choose to hike, this interpretive trail is a perfect place to start.

Plantation. Local planters stored their crops in the warehouse before they were shipped across the Atlantic to England.

The park was opened in its present form in 1980 to preserve this unique coastal environment, and has served as a model for all of Virginia's state parks in developing resource management plans.

All the trails begin at the Visitors Center,

(continued on page 79)

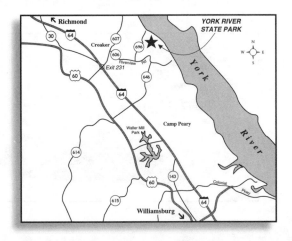

York River State Park

☞   From Richmond or Newport News – Take I-64 to Exit-231 for Croaker on **Route 607 north**. At Croaker, turn **right** on **Riverview Road (Route 606)**. Take this less than one mile to **York River Park Road (Route 696)** and turn **left**. Follow **York River Park Road** to the **Visitors Center**. Parking available.

MILES   DIRECTIONS

0.0   **START** at the **York River Park Visitors Center**. The **WOODSTOCK POND TRAIL** begins on the far east side of the Visitors Center. Follow this trail past the picnic area into the woods, where it loops around **Woodstock Pond**.

0.3   Pass the beginning of the Mattaponi Trail. Continue traveling along the **WOODSTOCK POND TRAIL**.

0.8   Pass the other end of the Mattaponi Trail. Continue **straight** on the **WOODSTOCK POND TRAIL**.

0.9   Woodstock Pond Trail loops around to the right and heads back to the Visitors Center at this point. Go **straight** on **BACKBONE TRAIL**.

2.2   Turn **left** on **RIVERVIEW TRAIL**.

2.3   Turn **right** at this gate to continue on **RIVERVIEW TRAIL**. At this point, the trail begins to narrow.

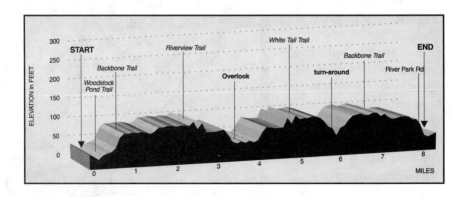

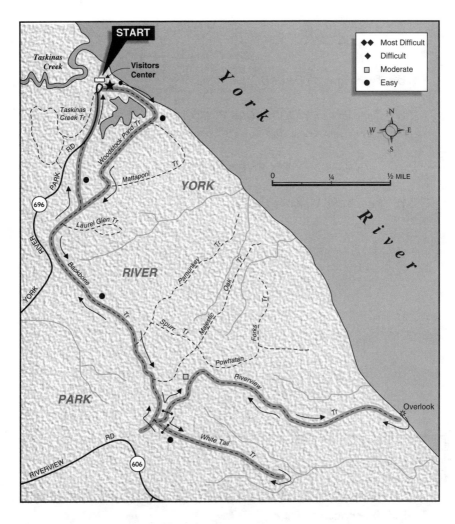

2.8   This narrow singletrack turns into a sandy jeep trail the rest
      of the way to the river.

3.7   Reach the **York River**. After checking out the great view of the
      river, turn around and head back along **RIVERVIEW TRAIL** to
      White Tail Trail.

5.3   Reach **Backbone Trail**. Immediately turn **hard left** on **WHITE
      TAIL TRAIL**.

5.9   Come to the end of White Tail Trail. This is a more wooded trail
      along the ridge of one of the park's many hillsides. It is mostly

a hard-packed dirt trail with a few fun hills. **Turn around** and return to Backbone Trail.

6.5   Turn **right** on **BACKBONE TRAIL**.

7.8   Bear **left** on **WOODSTOCK POND TRAIL**, heading toward York River Park Road and the Visitors Center.

8.1   Turn **right** on **YORK RIVER PARK ROAD**.

8.3   Reach the **Visitors Center**.

Ride Information

Trail Maintenance Hotline:
   York River State Park   (804) 566-3036
                                        (804) 786-1712
Cost:
   Small parking fee
Schedule:
   Open 8:00 A.M. until dusk, year-round
Maps:
   USGS maps: Gressitt, VA
   ADC map: Virginia Peninsula road map
   York River State Park trail map

(continued from page 75)

high on the banks of the York River. Not all trails in the park are open to bicyclists, so be careful to stay only on designated routes. The Woodstock Pond Trail, which is open to bicycles, follows a dirt road around the pond into the park before joining

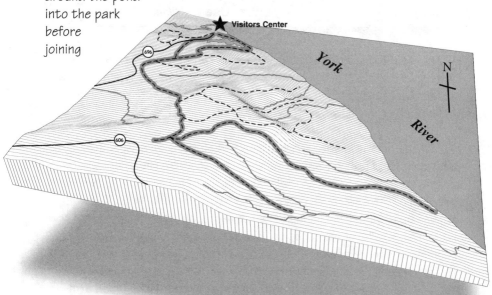

up with Backbone Trail—a flat dirt pathway that leads cyclists to each of the park's other trails. The other two trails open to bikes are the Riverview Trail and White Tail Trail.

Riverview Trail is one of the park's more challenging trails. Narrow and sandy, this singletrack winds its way through the park's forest toward the high banks of the river. Ivy and moss growing from the trees add to the thickness of the greenery all the way to a spectacular view overlooking the river. Take some time to climb down the steep cliffs, eroded and beaten by the river, and you may possibly find fossils of ancient fish and mammals.

White Tail Trail leads you through the woods along the ridge on one of the park's many hillsides. This trail is more of a hard-packed, dirt forest road. Though it is mostly flat, it has a few quick descents.

8. Petersburg National Battlefield

Start: *Visitors Center*	**Terrain:** *Dirt trails, singletrack*
Length: *6 miles of trails*	**Riding Time:** *1 – 2 hours*
Rating: *Easy*	**Other Uses:** *Hiking*

Mountain biking at Petersburg National Battlefield Park used to conjure thoughts of well maintained gravel or paved trails along an interpretive route of signs and exhibits—nothing very exciting. Upon further inspection, however, this proved not to be the case.

The park is a wonderfully preserved site of American history, maintaining and protecting the very ground on which the largest battle and the longest siege of the Civil War occurred. Nearly 70,000 Americans died in the Petersburg area during its 9½-month siege. Reasons for such high casualties ranged from attacks, counterattacks, artillery and mortar shells, sharpshooting, disease, and the ultimate fate of becoming prisoners of war.

General Grant firmly believed the key to taking Richmond was first to take Petersburg. If Petersburg were captured, the Union army could cut off all of Richmond's railroad lines and roadways so vital to the Confederate Capital's shipments of supplies and food. Many believed that if Richmond fell, the war would come to an end.

Grant's Union forces began arriving in mid-June 1864, and would not fully smother the Confederate army for another 9½ miserable months. After outnumbering Lee's cold, hungry, and exhausted soldiers, Grant ordered an all-out assault on April 2. Lee's army collapsed, and one week later, at Appomattox Court House, Lee surrendered; the war was over.

Today, Petersburg National Battlefield Park offers enough wooded trails open to bicycling that one would have to make plans *not* to ride to study its historical exhibits. Backroads and trails with such names as Attack Road and Encampment Trail take you cycling past massive Civil War earthworks and through some of the dense forest that was once an open field of war. These trails are exciting and scenic and add a new dimension to off-road cycling. One day is not enough to hike all the trails in this park, however on a

Cannons stand as monuments to the battles fought here in Petersburg.

bike, you should have no worries about exploring each new off-road battlefield route.

Be sure, though, not to get too carried away on these great off-road trails; there is so much else worth seeing at this park. One such sight is the massive crater left by a federal attack (a 511-foot-long tunnel and four tons of gunpowder were used to blow up a Confederate battery). The resulting hole was nearly 170 feet long, 60 feet wide, and 30 feet deep. Unfortunately for the Union army, this attack, which took one month to prepare, turned out to be a horrible failure. After blasting the Confederate battery with the massive charge, Union troops dove right into the crater, rather than going around it, and were thereby trapped. Confederate troops then launched a counterattack and inflicted more than 4,000 casualties on the federal forces. There would be much more fighting

(continued on page 86)

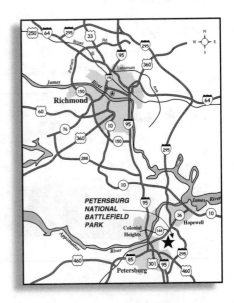

Petersburg National Battlefield

☞   **From I-95 at Petersburg** – Take the **Washington Street East (Route 36) exit** into **Petersburg.** Go approximately 2½ miles east on **Route 36** to the **Petersburg National Battlefield Park** entrance on the right. Follow the entrance road through the toll gate to the parking lot at the **Visitors Center.**

— NOTE —

All of these trails connect, at some point or another, with Siege Road (paved). Leave your car at the Visitors Center and ride the bike lane along Siege Road to each of these trails. Or, if you prefer, drive your car to the different parking areas along Siege Road and ride to the nearest off-road trail of your choice. Parking areas along Siege Road are shown on the map as small, black semicircles.

*The 3D profile map is a profile of **SIEGE ROAD** from the Visitors Center to the end of the park at Crater Road. Because there are so many individual trails weaving through this park, it would be unreasonable to create a directional route. Instead, each of these trails is described individually, and it is left up to the reader to choose which trails to ride. By mapping the profile of Siege Road (which has a bike route on it), this gives the reader a cross-section of the park and hopefully some sense of the park's ups and downs.*

TRAIL DESCRIPTIONS

Friend Trail

0.7 miles long. If you're riding into the park from the Visitors Center, this is the first trail you will come across. Friend Trail starts on

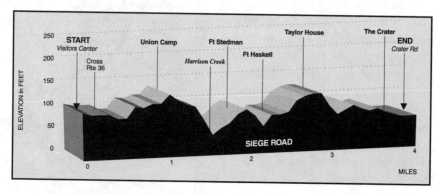

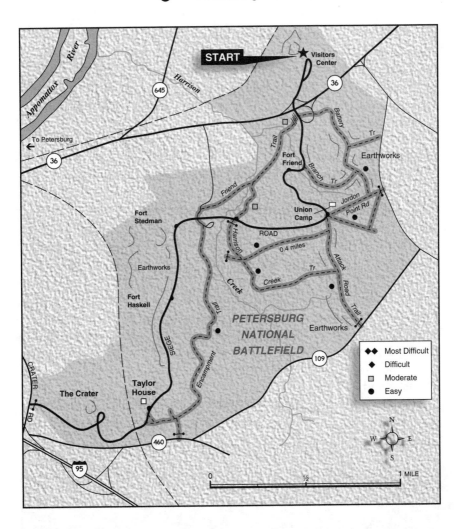

the right side of Siege Road, just across the bridge over Route 36. If you pass the traffic circle, you've gone too far. The trail dives down a set of steps into the battlefield wilderness and rambles along a picturesque, wooded trail past Battery 8. (Black U.S. troops captured this battery and renamed it Fort Friend for a large Friend House nearby. After it was captured, Fort Friend served as an artillery position during the siege of Petersburg.) Shortly after crossing Harrison Creek, this trail ends on a one-lane paved road. Turn left on this road to get back to Siege Road.

Encampment Trail

1.5 miles long. This trail begins from the maintenance area just off Siege Road. There is a sign here pointing into the woods for this trail.

The trail is mostly a single-lane jeep trail that winds through the woods toward the site of the old Taylor Farm. The farm, located on a ridge overlooking land west of the Taylor House, was quickly taken by troops at the start of the siege. During the battle of the Crater, Union troops lined up nearly 200 pieces of artillery on this ridge and fired down upon Confederate troops.

Harrison Creek Trail

1.0 mile long. There is a small parking area on Siege Road where you can enter this trail. Harrison Creek Trail crosses the road at this point and takes you through the woods along a National Historic Route. The short section of trail north of Siege Road is a fun, winding singletrack along the creek that will challenge anyone's skills. South of Siege Road the trail widens and allows for a more leisurely ramble through the forest.

During the siege, Confederate forces were driven back to Harrison Creek, where they dug in and held their line for two days. Later, in the last month of battle, Lee launched one last offensive—the Battle of Fort Stedman—and Lee's troops were stopped cold along this creek.

Attack Road

0.5 miles long. This old, dirt road connects Route 109 to Siege Road within the park. Harrison Creek Trail and the unnamed service road

Ride Information

Trail Maintenance Hotline:

Petersburg National Battlefield   (804) 732-3531

Cost:

$2.00 admission fee at front gate

Schedule:

Open 8:00 A.M. to dusk, year-round

Maps:

USGS maps: Petersburg, VA; Prince George, VA
ADC map: Petersburg & Vicinity road map
National Park Service Battlefield trail map

Cycling through the battlefield wilderness.

south of Siege Road intersect with Attack Road and lead to the Union Camp and Battery 9. Attack Road is lined on either side with heavy earthworks, which were built large and high to guard against a Confederate attack on the Union encampment.

Jordon Point Road

0.3 miles long. This dirt road and the other two roads, which together make a triangle, create what was an important supply route between Meade Station and the Union Camp. Meade Station provided a vital link along the City Point and Army Rail Line, which brought the Union Army supplies and medical equipment from City Point. This link ultimately secured Union victory over Lee's troops as it allowed for regular shipments of supplies. Lee's army, meanwhile, grew cold and hungry over the 9½-month siege and fell to Grant's well equipped army.

Branch Trail

0.3 miles long. Branch Trail and Battery Trail are very similar. Both trails wind through the thick Petersburg Battlefield forest, weaving around massive trenches and earthworks set up by the Union Army. Some of the earthworks are so high they cast shadows on the trail. Branch Trail takes you from Jordon Point Road to Siege Road, where you can follow the bike trail back to the Visitors Center.

Battery Trail

0.7 miles long. Battery Trail, like Branch Trail, weaves around the massive earthworks constructed by Union troops during the 9½-month siege. This area is called Battery 9, where black U.S. troops captured this position on the first day of fighting and held it throughout the entire siege. From Jordon Point Road, Battery Trail takes you all the way back to the entrance road next to Route 36. The trailhead is opposite the trailhead for Friend Trail.

Civil War cannons guard the ruins of the old Taylor House.

(continued from page 81)

before this siege would end.

The trails in this park are well maintained and don't represent a very high level of difficulty. They are open to the public, but are not meant for aggressive use. Ride gently on these historic paths and, by all means, stay on the designated trails. The Civil War earthworks are very fragile and can easily be scarred and damaged if ridden on. Take care of this National Historic Site and preserve it for the future.

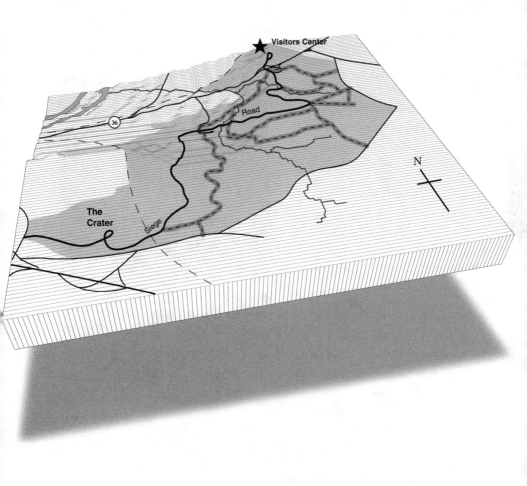

9. Pocahontas State Park

Start: *Park Office/Info Center* **Terrain:** *Hard-packed dirt trails*
Length: *6.1 miles* **Riding Time:** *1 – 1½ hours*
Rating: *Easy* **Other Uses:** *Hiking, Horseback*

Pocahontas is a familiar name associated with early colonial America. According to legend, this younger daughter of Powhatan (chief of a federation of Algonquian Indian tribes living in the Tidewater region) saved Captain John Smith's life. As the story goes, Powhatan's warriors captured Smith, the self-appointed leader of the first Jamestown settlers, and sentenced him to death. Pocahontas, whose real name was Matoaka, pleaded with her father to spare him, and Smith, by a relenting Chief Powhatan, was allowed to go free.

Legend holds that as a young girl, Pocahontas often visited Jamestown. As she grew older she would bring food to the settlers and warn the colonists of possible Indian attacks. Later, as a result of the settler's kindness toward her, she chose to convert to Christianity, and changed her name to Rebecca. While visiting Jamestown, she met John Rolfe, an early settler noted as the first commercial tobacco grower. They married on April 5, 1614, had a child named Thomas, then sailed to England for a visit. She was one of the first Native Americans to visit London. During her stay, however, Pocahontas contracted smallpox and died in March 1617.

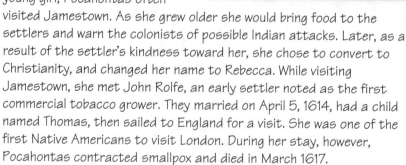

The name Pocahontas means "playful one," which might explain why the com- monwealth of Virginia chose the name for this state park. Unlike many other parks in Virginia, the forest

Cycling past Beaver Lake Dam.

land surrounding Pocahontas is deeded to the park, not the state, which gives recreational activities priority over other land uses such as timber production. This serves this populated region in Virginia well, as Pocahontas State Park and its surrounding state forest are within just 20 minutes of both Richmond and Petersburg.

Because of its proximity to these growing metropolitan communities, Pocahontas has been one of the state's busiest state parks since the Civilian Conservation Corps built the park's first recreation area in 1934. Today, hiking, swimming, horseback riding, and the latest addition—off-road bicycling—are all offered within the park's 7,604 acres. Along with the many trails that already exist for hiking and horseback riding, Pocahontas State Park recently developed the five-mile Old Mill Bicycle Trail, which winds through the woods around the 24-acre Beaver Lake.

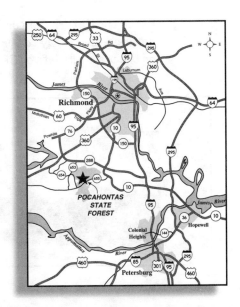

The Old Mill Bicycle Trail

(continued on page 93)

Pocahontas State Park

From Richmond – Take I-95 south to Exit-6. Follow **Route 10 west** approximately 7 miles to **Beach Road (Route 655)**. Turn **left** on **Route 655**, go approximately 4 miles, and follow the signs. Turn **right** into the park. The park office is just up the road.

MILES   DIRECTIONS

0.0   START at the **Park Office and Information Center**.
      BOTTOMS FOREST ROAD begins across Park Road, opposite
      the parking lot.

0.5   Bear **right**, traveling on **BOTTOMS FOREST ROAD**. Signs
      along the trail will direct you. This forest road, like many of the
      others along this ride, is a wide, hard-packed trail canopied by
      the forest's thick growth of hardwoods and pine.

1.2   Reach the main loop. At this trail split, turn **right** on **OLD
      MILL BICYCLE TRAIL**. Follow the **white arrows** painted on the
      ground. These arrows point you in a counterclockwise direction
      around the loop.

2.1   Cross a little bridge over the creek past Beaver Lake dam.
      (This is a very scenic area.)

2.3   Reach the **Nature Center**. You must pass in front of the
      nature center (stay to the left of the parking lot) to remain
      on the trail. Turn **left** on **CROSSTIE FOREST ROAD**.

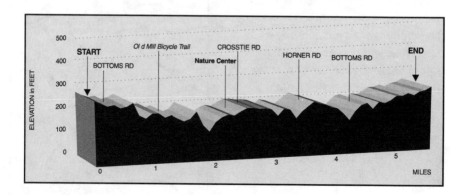

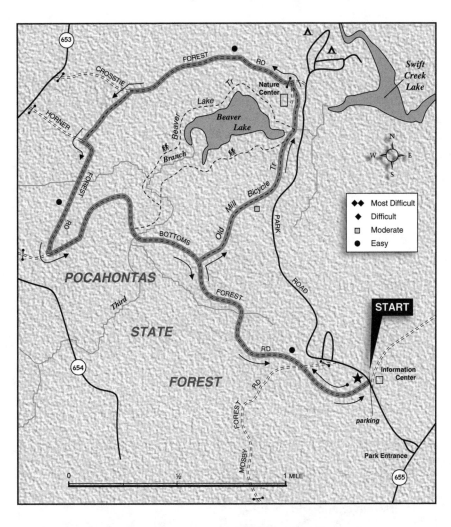

3.1   Bear **left,** continuing on **CROSSTIE FOREST ROAD.**

3.3   Follow along this forest road through a tunnel of tall loblolly
      pines. Timber harvests were, at one time, common in
      Pocahontas State Forest. Today, much of the pine growing
      along the trail was planted and has since reached impressive
      heights.

3.4   Turn **left** on **HORNER FOREST ROAD.**

4.1   Turn **left** on **BOTTOMS FOREST ROAD.**

4.7   Pass Beaver Lake Trail on the left. (Bikes are not allowed on this trail.)

5.0   Reach the end of the loop at Old Mill Bicycle Trail. Bear **right** at this split, following **BOTTOMS FOREST ROAD** through the woods back to the start of the ride.

6.1   Arrive back at the parking lot.

Ride Information

Trail Maintenance Hotline:

Pocahontas State Park	(804) 796-4255
Dept. of Conservation & Recreation	(804) 786-1712

Cost:

Small parking, camping, and pool fee

Schedule:

Open 8:00 A.M. until dusk daily, year-round

Maps:

USGS maps: Chesterfield, VA; Beach, VA
ADC map: Richmond & Vicinity road map
Pocahontas State Park trail map

(continued from page 89)

begins from the Information Center near the park entrance and follows Bottoms Forest Road into Pocahontas State Forest. The terrain is rolling and many of the trails are wide and inviting, allowing cyclists of all abilities to enjoy the wooded environment of a state forest. Upon reaching the first split in the trail, turn right, following the white arrows painted on the ground. This will lead you counterclockwise

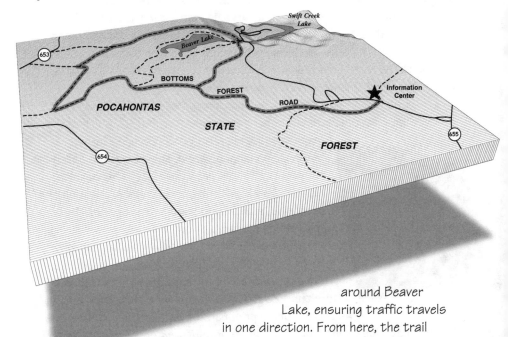

around Beaver Lake, ensuring traffic travels in one direction. From here, the trail narrows and winds beneath a leafy canopy of a tall hardwood and pine forest. In under one mile you will cross a small footbridge past the dam and climb a short, steep hill to the Nature Center. Bear left around the Nature Center on Crosstie Forest Road and continue along the rolling forest roads in the forest. Signs along the route point the way. The only challenge Pocahontas State Park and the surrounding forest land offer is the difficulty off-road cyclists may have in leaving for home, as there are many more miles of dirt forest roads that network through the forest.

10. Belle Isle

Start: *Belle Isle parking lot*	**Terrain:** *Dirt path, rugged singletrack*
Length: *Many miles of trails*	**Riding Time:** *Varies with distance*
Rating: *Easy to Difficult*	**Other Uses:** *Hiking, hanging out, dogs*

Belle Isle, part of the James River Park System and one of Richmond's most popular city parks, is located in the heart of Virginia's state capital. This 54-acre island in the middle of the James River attracts thousands of visitors annually. Its high cliff walls, rushing rapids, stone ruins, and fascinating history together make this island one of the most unique mountain biking spots in Virginia.

Once a Native American fishing village, Belle Isle provided bountiful river harvests such as the American freshwater mussel, which still exist along the banks of the James. During America's colonial period, the island was called Broad Rock Island because of its large granite walls. It had a general store, crops growing on the east side, and a ferry that transported folks to and from the island.

The Civil War brought to the island a gruesome purpose. The northeastern section was used as a prisoner-of-war camp for captured Union soldiers. More than 20,000 prisoners were sent here, and at one time as many as 8,000 Union prisoners of war were detained in the island's notorious tent city. Thousands of captured soldiers sent to the island subsequently died of dysentery and disease.

During the Industrial Revolution, iron works came to Belle Isle. Ruins of the old iron rolling, milling, and slitting manufactory still exist on the east side along the main trail. This plant ran on water power and slave labor in the early nineteenth century and produced such products as horseshoes, nails, spikes, copper pots, and bowls.

Also during this time, a man named James Bell built a race track on the flat land of then Broad Rock Island's east side. Hundreds arrived nightly to what they called Bell's Island to gamble and watch the races. It is reported that when James Bell left the island, several women from Richmond attempted to restore the island's image by renaming it with a more refined French title of *Belle*

Cyclists cross Belle Isle's footbridge.

Isle, which means in English, "the good island."

Today Belle Isle is used exclusively as an outdoor recreation area for Richmonders weary of the city's skyscrapers and pavement. The Belle Isle Footbridge transports visitors from Tredegar Street over the James River to Belle Isle's eastern flatland. The main trail around the island starts to the right of the bridge. This main trail makes a one-mile loop through the island, passing many of the historical artifacts left to ruin. For cyclists, this path is short and can be crowded on nice days and week-ends. However, if you spin up the high hills of the inner island, you'll find a network of singletrack trails crisscrossing the island's high ground.

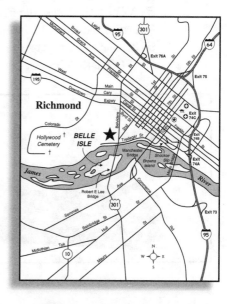

These trails, though not yet closed to bikes, are not

(continued on page 99)

Belle Isle

☞   From I-95 through Downtown Richmond – Take **Exit-74B** to **Franklin Street**. Turn **right** on **Franklin Street**. At the first light, turn **left** on **14th Street**. Go one block and turn **right** on **Main Street** (one way) at the light. *Follow signs to Belle Isle and the Valentine Museum.* Turn **left** on **5th Street**. Go two blocks, cross over the Downtown Expressway, and turn **left** on **Byrd Street**. Turn **right** at the Federal Reserve Building on **7th Street**. At the fountain, bear **right** on **Tredegar Street**, pass the Valentine Riverside Museum, and park at the **Belle Isle Parking Lot**.

MILES   DIRECTIONS

0.0   **START** at the **Belle Isle Parking Lot** next to the Valentine Riverside Museum. Turn **right**, heading west, on **TREDEGAR STREET** to the footbridge ramp. Cycle up the ramp and cross the **FOOTBRIDGE** over the James River.

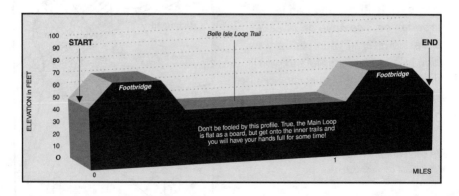

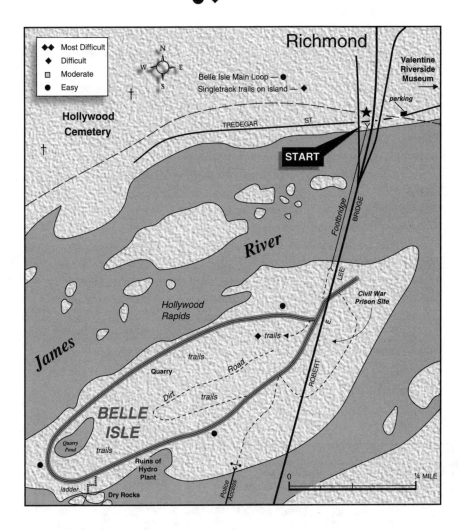

0.25   Reach **BELLE ISLE.** The footbridge drops you onto the island. The main trail around the island starts to the right of the bridge.

★ 0.3   Reach the main bike route around the island. You may circle the island in either direction.

1.2   Reach the end of the loop. To return to the car, take the footbridge back over the James River to the parking lot.

1.5   Reach the parking lot.

★ If you want to explore the hilly, singletrack trails on the island, go straight at this junction and climb the dirt hill toward the center of the island. This hill is a short, steep climb. Once you're up this hill, there are a number of trails that you may ride on. Many are quite difficult and some are downright hard. There are enough trails on the island to spend an afternoon exploring. The park service warns that many of the trails on Belle Isle are steep and rocky and should be treated with caution.

As you pedal around the main loop of Belle Isle, you may notice there are a number of places to access the singletrack trails on the island. There are also a number of areas posted with signs reading, "No Bikes." Please don't ride in these areas.

When the weather is dry, another fun spot for some crazy cycling is the dry rocks area on the island's south side. Walk across the metal walkway from the main trail, then climb down a ladder to the rocks. This is not the place to come expecting to ride with much speed, but with lots of technical bike-handling skills, cyclists can maneuver from one rock to the next without falling into the river.

Remember, on the weekends and holidays Belle Isle gets very crowded. Be extremely cautious when riding here and, by all means, keep the speeds down.

Ride Information

Trail Maintenance Hotline:

City of Richmond Parks & Rec.	(804) 780-5733
James River Park Visitors Center	(804) 780-5311

Schedule:

Open daylight to dusk, year-round

Maps:

USGS maps:	Richmond, VA
ADC map:	Richmond & Vicinity road map

Belle Isle Interpretive Guide and Trail Map

(continued from page 95)

recommended to cyclists by the park service because of their difficulty level and danger. Trails on the inner island are not maintained and should be approached with great caution and responsibility. Ride only on the inner trails and avoid the cliffs on the island's north side near the Hollywood Rapids. Remember to be careful, and you're guaranteed a great ride on Belle Isle.

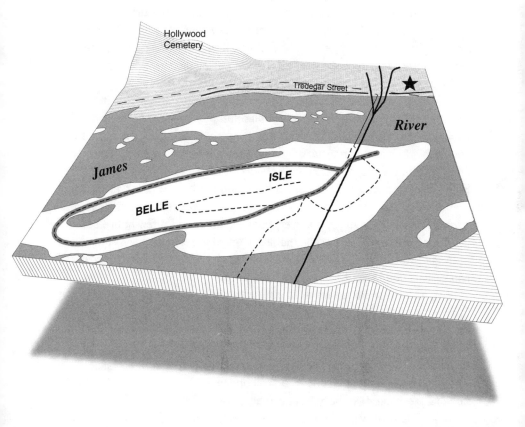

11. Poor Farm Park

Start: *Archery Range Trailhead* **Terrain:** *Hilly singletrack*
Length: *5 miles total* **Riding Time:** *1 – 1½ hours*
Rating: *Moderate to Difficult* **Other Uses:** *Hiking, nature tours*

Richmond's mountain bikers know that finding good singletrack in the area is somewhat difficult. Like many of Virginia's urban areas, Richmond is far removed from the rugged hills of the Allegheny Mountains and vast public land of the state's national forests. Richmond's terrain, in fact, is typically flat to rolling, at best, and much of the surrounding land is privately owned. But like many other urban areas hard-pressed for singletrack, there are exceptions. While the Richmond area might, at first, appear to be a dry well for off-road riding, upon closer inspection, cyclists will find a spring of singletrack delight in a regional park called Poor Farm, just west of nearby Ashland.

The park is located next to a middle school, and within its boundaries are playing fields, volleyball sand pits, soccer fields, picnic tables, and an amphitheater. But don't let these leisurely amenities fool you. Behind this regional-park facade, through the woods and down the hill from the playing fields, lies a network of off-road cycling adventure. Hills, steep trails, and fast descents abound in this woodland region.

Granted, this is a small regional park, so don't expect days of endless exploration. It is, however, possible to spend a few hours pedaling Poor Farm's wooded trails, honing that singletrack savvy. And, if you manage to cross Stagg Creek, miles of singletrack beneath the power lines await your tread.

One of the best ways to get onto the trail system at Poor Farm Park is to enter at the Archery Range trailhead. From the gravel parking lot at the end of the park entrance road, ride through the open gate, pedaling past the volleyball sand pits toward the soccer fields. Just beyond the sand pits, on the right side of the field, there is a large wooden sign hanging in front of a trail opening. This is the trailhead for the orange-blazed Archery Range Trail.

This trail will lead you downhill toward Stagg Creek, where you can go one of two ways. Turning right at the end of the descent allows you to continue following the loop around the archery course. A left turn will take you on a narrow trail marked with blue and

Challenging singletrack near Virginia's capital city.

white blazes along the creek. Both of these trails are challenging, with plenty of obstacles and steep hills guaranteed to keep you on your toes.

Besides these two main trails, you can branch off on one of the side trails to explore a little deeper into the park. Some of these trails are longer than others and have different degrees of difficulty.

The best way to approach cycling in this park, though, is to not worry about following specific routes. Rather, pedal your way into the woods on one of these many trails and just start riding, making up loops on your own.

Please be aware, of course, that this is a regional park open to all types of trail users. On most days there are certain to be other people enjoying the trails, particularly hikers and nature tour enthusiasts. This isn't strictly a mountain bike park, so be sure to ride responsibly and always yield the right of way to other trail users.

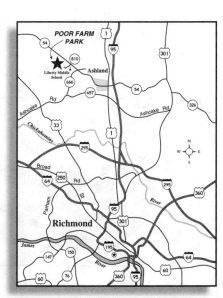

Poor Farm Park

☞   From Richmond – Take I-95 north to Ashland. Exit on **Route 54 west** at Ashland. Follow **Route 54 west** approximately 5 miles to Liberty Middle School. Turn **left** on **Route 810**, pass Liberty Middle School, and follow the signs for **Poor Farm Park**. Route 810 ends at a **gravel parking lot**. Park here.

MILES   DIRECTIONS

Orange Loop/Archery Range Trail

0.0   **START** from the **gravel parking lot** at the end of the park entrance road. Go around the gate, past the volleyball sand pits, toward the soccer fields. The trailhead for the Archery Range Trail (orange blaze) is on the right side of the field, past the sand pits.

0.2   Reach the wooden sign marking the trailhead for the **ARCHERY RANGE TRAIL (orange blaze)**. Follow this into the woods and start descending an old jeep road.

0.4   Reach Stagg Creek at the bottom of this descent. Turn **right** along the creek, following the **ARCHERY RANGE TRAIL (orange blaze)**. Left leads you along the Blue/White Trail.

0.6   Heading away from Stagg Creek, cross over a small wooden footbridge.

0.85   Pass a narrow, singletrack trail on the left. This trail weaves

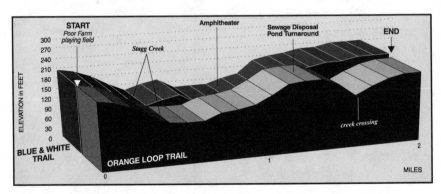

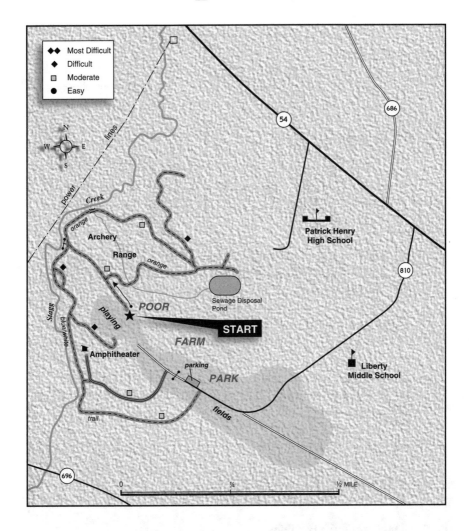

through the trees along another hillside before coming to a dead-end, three-tenths of a mile away.

0.9 At the top of this climb, turn **hard right**, continuing to follow the **orange blazes** of the ARCHERY RANGE TRAIL. Start descending to a small creek. Straight takes you to the Sewage Disposal Pond.

1.2 Cross a small wooden footbridge at the bottom of the descent. Now you must climb out of this wedge.

1.3 Reach the top of the climb and turn **left** on the JEEP TRAIL.

This takes you uphill toward the playing fields to the start of the loop.

1.4   Reach the playing fields and the end of the orange-blazed Archery Range Trail.

Blue/White Trail

0.0   **START** again from the trailhead for the **ARCHERY RANGE TRAIL (orange blaze)** on the right side of the playing fields. Follow the trail into the woods and start descending the old jeep road.

0.4   Reach Stagg Creek at the bottom of this descent. Turn **left** on the **BLUE/WHITE TRAIL,** following the creek south toward the amphitheater. The first section of this trail is all singletrack, as it travels along Stagg Creek. At times the trail is rugged and steep. This is a great trail for technical riding.

0.6   Pass a trail that heads left up the hill. This trail becomes very steep before exiting into the playing fields. Continue **straight** along the creek.

Ride Information

Trail Maintenance Hotline:

    Hanover Visitor Information Center   (804) 752-6766
    Liberty Middle School   (804) 752-6020

Schedule:

    Open daylight to dark, year-round

Maps:

    USGS maps: Hanover Academy, VA

0.75   Pass the amphitheater on the left. Continue on the trail.

0.8   Bear **left** with the trail, climbing the outer edge of the park
        toward the park road. This is a fairly easy ascent from the
        creek. Be careful not to get jammed between the trees and
        the fence along this trail.

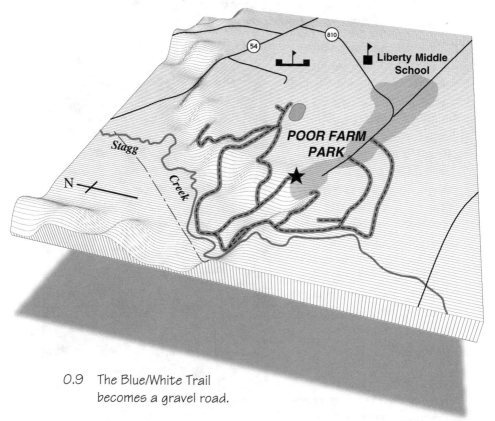

0.9   The Blue/White Trail
        becomes a gravel road.

1.2   Reach the park road. Turn **left** on the park road and head
        back to the parking lot.

1.3   Reach the playing fields and the end of this trail.

The mileage for this ride is deceptively low. While there aren't miles and
miles of trails, the trails that are here take you in many different
directions, creating many different routes. It's easy to spend an hour or
two tooling around at Poor Farm. If you want to work on some technical skills, riding at Poor Farm Park is the place to come and practice.

12. Cumberland State Forest

Start: *Bear Creek Lake S.P.*	**Terrain:** *Flat to rolling dirt roads, jeep trails*
Length: *40-50 miles total*	**Riding Time:** *Varies with distance*
Rating: *Easy to Moderate*	**Other Uses:** *Hiking, timber harvest*

Between the Appalachian and Blue Ridge Mountains to the west and the flat coastal plains to the east lies Virginia's Piedmont region, characterized by its gently rolling hills and quiet valleys. This is an area of few extremes, where the terrain is neither hilly nor flat and pines, cedars, and hardwoods grow side by side. Land from Manassas to Danville makes up Virginia's Piedmont, and just like Virginia's mountains and coast, off-road bicycling has found its way into this central region.

The majority of accessible mountain biking terrain in the Piedmont region is primarily within Virginia's

The forest has many uses. Timber is one of its greatest resources.

state forests. The Virginia Division of Forestry administers four state forests in the Piedmont region: Cumberland, Appomattox-Buckingham, Prince Edward-Gallion, and Pocahontas State Forests, all of which comprise nearly 50,000 acres. This provides the largest publicly owned land open to mountain biking east of the Blue Ridge Mountains.

While mountain biking is popular in the state forests, Virginia's forests are primarily managed for such things as watershed protection, timber production, and research. For example, several natural areas in the different state forests are reserved exclusively for research. These natural areas are intended for use as outdoor

Plan to stay home during hunting season.

laboratories for students of ecology, botany, and other natural sciences. In these areas, timber cutting and recreation (such as mountain biking) are strictly off limits.

While the natural areas are safeguarded from overuse, there are many areas in Virginia's state forests that are specifically designed for public use. Within each forest is a state park that provides a variety of outdoor activities, from camping and picnicking to swimming, boating, hiking, and cycling.

Cumberland State Forest is singled out in this guide as the representative state forest. It is also the headquarters for Virginia's Piedmont state forests. The other three state forests mentioned are similar in size and terrain, and all have many miles of dirt forest roads and trails ideal for off-road bicycling.

Cumberland State Forest is situated in the heart of Virginia, less than

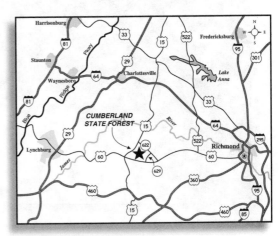

(continued on page 111)

Cumberland State Forest

☞   **From Richmond** – Take **U.S. 60 west** from Richmond approximately 40 miles to **Cumberland State Forest**. U.S. 60 travels through the forest. Turn **right** off U.S. 60 just east of Cumberland Courthouse on **Route 622**. Take Route 622 north 4.5 miles, then turn **left** on **Route 629**. Route 629 leads you into **Bear Creek Lake State Park,** where you can park. Parking, information, camping, toilets, and showers available.

START at **Bear Creek Lake State Park**. Bear Creek Lake State Park is a small state park with a 40-acre lake as its main attraction. Camping, picnicking, hiking, fishing, and swimming are some of the popular activities here. There is also a modern bathhouse and a full-service concession area. Leave your car at the lake and hit the forest roads and trails for a good day's bike ride, then return for a cool swim and hot shower.

(Note: Because Cumberland State Forest has so many individual forest roads and trails suitable for cycling, it would be unreasonable to create a single loop. Instead, cyclists are encouraged to use the forest map provided and select your own routes through the state forest. For this reason, there is no profile map available.)

Most of the roads are maintained forest service roads used by loggers harvesting timber. There are countless dead-end trails and dry-weather roads that are gated, all of which branch off the main forest roads.

Share the road!

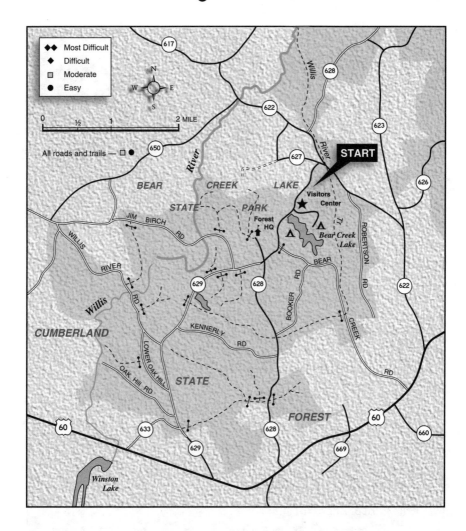

Most of these trails are seeded to reduce erosion and improve game habitat. They travel into the woods sometimes up to one half of a mile before ending. At that point, just turn around and head back to the road. These trails provide a wonderful diversion from the main forest roads and bring cyclists much closer to the forest's natural setting.

Note on the map the shaded area above Route 622. Cumberland State Forest continues well north of this road. In fact, only about half of the state forest is mapped in this guide. Be sure to get the Virginia Department of Forestry's *Guide to Virginia's Piedmont State Forests* if you wish to travel further north (Virginia Division of Parks and Recreation, 804-786-2132). In addition to Cumberland State Forest, the Virginia Department of Forestry's guide also provides detailed maps of

Appomattox-Buckingham State Forest, Prince Edward-Gallion State Forest, and Pocahontas State Forest. Each of these four different state forests have many miles of great forest roads and trails suitable for mountain biking. For a bit more information on each of these state forests, turn to the **Honorable Mentions** section, beginning on page 232, and see what they have to offer.

In most parts of Virginia, hunting season is from November 21 to January 7. The hunting season includes most game, including deer. Some game hunting, such as grouse, starts as early as October 15. During this time of year, please call the appropriate land managers *first* to find out exactly what days fall within hunting season for each region before heading out on the trails.

Ride Information

Trail Maintenance Hotline:

    Cumberland State Forest   *(804) 492-4121*
    Bear Creek Lake State Park   *(804) 492-4410*

Schedule:

    Open daylight to dark all year-round

Maps:

    USGS maps: *Gold Hill, VA; Hillcrest, VA*
                        Whiteville, VA
    Delorme: *Virginia Atlas & Gazetteer – Page 56 D–2*
    VA Dept of Forestry: Guide to VA State Forests map

(continued from page 107)

one hour west of Richmond. Its nearly 17,000 acres of flat-to-rolling terrain are filled with forest roads, dead-end trails, and dirt paths. Many of the dirt roads lead through scenic hardwood and pine forests and past the natural habitats of deer, turkey, quail, squirrels, rabbits, and raccoons. The areas, you will notice, that are absent of trees have been harvested by the state and sold as timber. The bare spots have been replanted, though, and will be closely monitored in the years

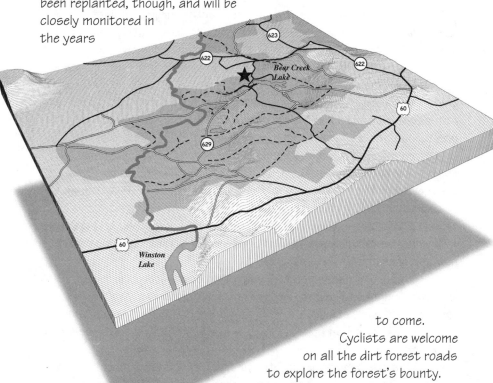

to come. Cyclists are welcome on all the dirt forest roads to explore the forest's bounty.

One note of caution to anyone venturing into the forests: please be aware that the state forests make up a significant portion of land open to public hunting in Central Virginia. Like the national forest land in Western Virginia's mountains, hunting is a popular sport. Be aware of hunting seasons and be careful not to get caught in the woods during a deer hunt.

13. Charlottesville Dirt Ride

Start: *Stony Point Elem School* **Terrain:** *Hilly dirt roads, paved roads*
Length: *20.3 miles*   **Riding Time:** *2 – 2½ hours*
Rating: *Moderate*   **Other Uses:** *Automobiles*

Charlottesville, located in the heart of Central Virginia amidst the rising foothills of the Blue Ridge Mountains, is a stately town of slightly more than 40,000 people. Home to such well-known Americans as Thomas Jefferson and James Monroe, Charlottesville has enjoyed a history of prominent figures who came to live and study within its rolling landscape. Thomas Jefferson's landmark mountaintop estate Monticello commands a breathtaking view of the rolling countryside and the prestigious University of Virginia he founded in 1819. "The University," as it is often referred to, is now home to more than 11,000 students.

The countryside of Charlottesville is a wonderful place to spend the day pedaling past wineries, old plantations, fields of dogwood, and, of course, horses, horses, horses. Not every off-road ride, as you will witness along these quiet backroads, needs be a mountainous adventure with white-knuckling descents and bone-jarring trails. A change every now and then can be very enjoyable.

Change of pace is precisely why this scenic loop is included. This ride was designed to showcase the treasures of Central Virginia while, for the most part, staying off-road. It's a great ride for the leisurely mountain biker with an appetite for the scenery and solitude of peaceful backroads.

The ride begins at the Stony Point Elementary School just off Route 20. Park your car in the school parking lot. You will travel up a quiet mountain road to the top of Charlottesville's Southwest Mountains before descending quickly toward the small town of Cismont. The Southwest Mountains have the highest peaks east of the Blue Ridge. Snacks and refreshments are available at the corner store along Route 231. Be careful along the next section of this ride on Route 22, as this is a bit more heavily traveled by cars.

Cruise through the equally small towns of Cobham and Cash Corner (food and drinks available) before heading back over the Southwest Mountains through Turkeysag Gap. Horse farms and colorful gardens provide the scenery all the way back to the

Thoroughbreds grace Charlottesville's horse country.

mountain. The rest of the ride is along more of the numerous backroads in this region, all of which are scenic, quiet, and peaceful—perfect for a leisurely ride through the countryside.

This may be the most off-road riding many could wish for. If you live in the Central Virginia region, especially near Charlottesville, you will be pleased to know there are miles and miles of backroads like the ones offered on this ride. Many of these paths pass through old farmland, past exquisite horse stables, and near Virginia's famous wineries. These types of rides bring you so much closer to the area's rural landscape than paved roads can deliver. So take some time to explore this off-road experience, and I'm sure you'll be pleased with your discoveries.

★ Check out the *Sugarloaf Mountain Ride* in the **Honorable Mentions** section—another beautiful ride along some of the peaceful backroads in the Charlottesville area.

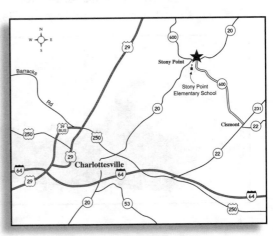

Charlottesville Dirt Ride

☞   From Charlottesville – Take **Route 20 north** for approximately
8 miles to **Stony Point Elementary School**. Park here. You can access
Route 20 from both I-64 and Route 250.

MILES   DIRECTIONS

0.0   START at **Stony Point Elementary School**. Parking available.
Turn **right** on ROUTE 20 (paved).

0.3   Turn **right** on **STONY POINT PASS (ROUTE 600)** (hard-
packed dirt and gravel). This road takes you through
Charlottesville's Southwest Mountains.

3.4   Reach the summit. There's a small clearing here, but no real
view except when the foliage is thin during winter. You may
also notice some trails heading into the woods on the left.
Tempting as it may be, these trails travel across private
property. Stick to the road.

4.2   Route 600 changes to pavement.

4.4   Route 600 changes back to dirt.

4.7   Reach the end of the descent. Pass a large horse stable on
the left.

5.7   Cross **Gordonsville Road (Route 231)**. Continue **straight**
along the paved road through **Cismont**. Snacks, Coke ma-

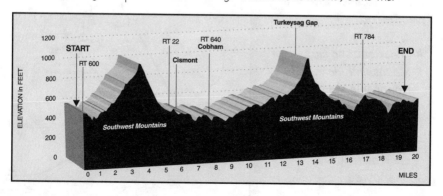

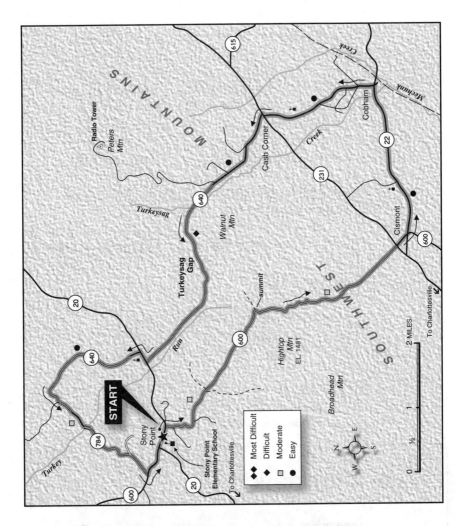

chine, refreshments at the Chevron gas station on this corner.

6.0   Turn **left** on **LOUISA ROAD (ROUTE 22)** (paved). Be careful of traffic along this road.

8.5   Arrive in the town of **Cobham**. Turn **left** on **ROUTE 640** (paved). This area showcases the magnificent horse farms and stables that make this area famous as you travel back toward the mountain along this flat, paved road.

10.5   Cross **Gordonsville Road (Route 231)**. Get some snacks or drinks at the **Cash Corner** store. Stay on **ROUTE 640** (paved).

12.0   Route 640 changes to dirt and gravel and begins climbing back over the Southwest Mountains. Check out the summit of Peters Mountain if you dare challenge the ascent.

13.3   Reach the summit and cross through **Turkeysag Gap**.

15.4   Turn **right** on **STONY POINT ROAD (ROUTE 20)** (paved). Bobbi's grocery store at this intersection.

15.6   Turn **left** on **GILBERT STATION ROAD (ROUTE 640)** (paved).

15.7   Start climbing (dirt).

16.8   Reach the summit of this climb.

17.5   **Bear left.** *Do not* turn right on Brocks Mill Road (dirt).

17.7   Turn **left** at this intersection on **ROUTE 784** (dirt). If you look to the left along this road you can see through the trees the Southwest Mountains that you crossed just a few miles

Ride Information

Trail Maintenance Hotline:

Not available

Schedule:

All roads open to the public year-round

Maps:

USGS maps:	Barboursville, VA; Keswick, VA
	Charlottesville East, VA
DeLorme:	VA Atlas & Gazetteer – Page 68 D–2

back.

18.2   Paved descent.

18.4   Cross a small bridge at the bottom of this descent (dirt).

19.7   Turn **left** at the stop sign on **ROUTE 600** (paved).

20.2   Go **straight** through the intersection of Route 20 and Route 600.

20.3   Reach the **Stony Point Elementary School**. This ride would be fun on one of those horses!

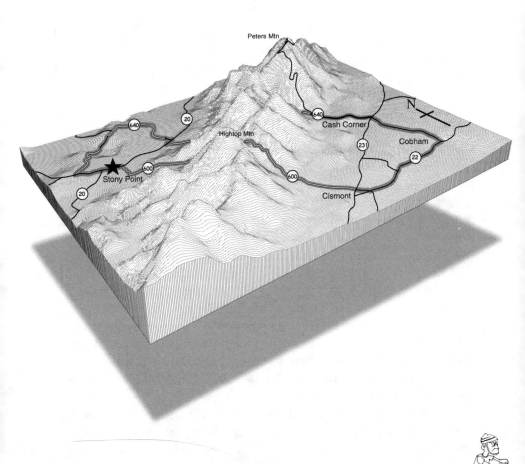

14. Great Falls National Park

Start: *Visitors Center*
Length: *6.8 miles*
Rating: *Moderate*

Terrain: *Rocky dirt trails; fire roads*
Riding Time: *1 – 1½ hours*
Other Uses: *Hiking, Horseback*

Great Falls is one of the United State's most popular national parks. How appropriate then for it to be located just 14 miles from our nation's capital. And what a thrill for cyclists to know that mountain biking is not only allowed at the park—it's welcome.

Along with hikers, historians, rock climbers, and kayakers, off-road cyclists come in droves to enjoy Great Falls' public resources. There are over five miles of designated trails to enjoy in this park, all of which conveniently intersect to create hours of off-road adventure. The trails vary in intensity, ranging from rolling forest roads beneath tall oaks and maples to steep, rocky singletrack overlooking the dramatic Mather Gorge. The park's unequaled beauty, proximity to Washington, and accessible trails combine to make Great Falls National Park Northern Virginia's most popular off-road cycling haven.

The ride begins at the Visitors Center parking lot and travels south along Old Carriage Road through the middle of the park. Old Carriage was used in the 1700s to carry settlers to their dwellings at Matildaville, ruins of which still stand today. This small town was developed by Henry Lee, a Revolutionary War hero and friend of George Washington's. Named after Lee's first wife, Matildaville lasted only three decades before fading into history.

The route bends deep into the park and travels up and down the rocky pass along Ridge Trail. During the winter months, breathtaking views of the gorge show through deciduous trees. The trail then descends quickly to the Potomac (another

Cyclists enjoy a break overlooking Great Falls.

great view) and follows along Difficult Run before heading north again back toward the start.

(continued on page 123)

Great Falls National Park

☞   **From the Capital Beltway (495)** – From **Exit-13** northwest of McLean, take **Route 193 (Georgetown Pike) west** toward **Great Falls.** Go approximately 4 miles, then turn **right** on **Old Dominion Drive.** Go 1 mile to the end of the **park entrance road** and park at the **Visitors Center.** Telephones, water, food, toilet, information available.

MILES   DIRECTIONS

0.0   START at **Great Falls Visitor Center.** Follow the **Horse/Biker trail** south along **Entrance Road.**

0.4   Bear **right** at the restrooms and go around the steel gate on **OLD CARRIAGE ROAD** (unpaved).

1.1   Bear **left** down the trail to **Sandy Landing.**

1.3   Arrive at **Sandy Landing.** A beautiful spot along the river, great for viewing Mather Gorge. You may also notice kayakers battling the rapids, while rock climbers scale the granite walls on the other side of the gorge. Return to **Old Carriage Road.**

1.5   Turn **left,** continuing on **OLD CARRIAGE ROAD.** Begin a steady uphill.

1.9   Turn **left** near the top of this climb on **RIDGE TRAIL.** Hang tough on this hilly, rocky trail.

2.7   Turn **left** after the steep descent on **DIFFICULT RUN TRAIL.**

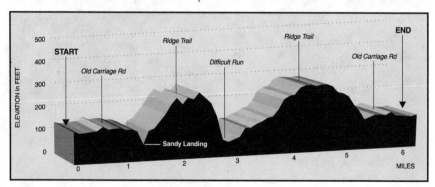

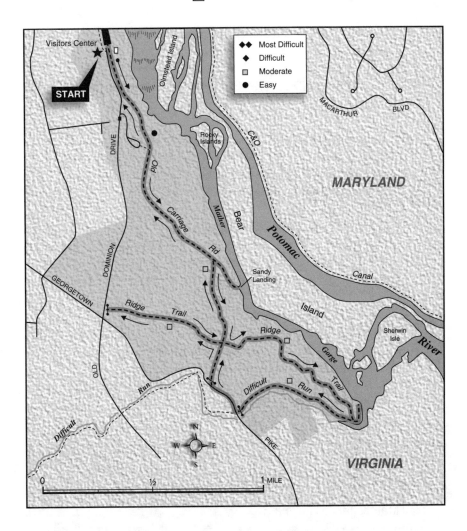

Head toward the Potomac.

2.9   Arrive at the **Potomac River**. This spot along the banks of the Potomac gives you a good view of Sherwin Island, where Mather Gorge and the Potomac River merge. Turn around and follow **DIFFICULT RUN TRAIL** west toward Georgetown Pike along Difficult Run Creek.

3.6   Turn **right** on **GEORGETOWN PIKE**. Be careful of traffic. Ride along the dirt shoulder.

3.8   Turn **right** on **OLD CARRIAGE ROAD**. This is the first dirt road you come to along Georgetown Pike. Go around the gate and begin climbing.

4.0   Turn **left** on **RIDGE TRAIL**. Follow this toward the entrance road.

4.7   Reach Great Falls' entrance road (Old Dominion Road). Turn around and continue back on **RIDGE TRAIL**. If you've had enough, turn right on the entrance road, heading back to the Visitors Center directly.

5.4   Turn **left** on **OLD CARRIAGE ROAD**.

6.4   Go through the gate at the beginning of Old Carriage Road and ride back to the parking lot at the Visitors Center.

6.8   Arrive back at the **Visitors Center** and parking lot. Take a moment after this ride to walk along some of the hiking trails from the Visitors Center. These trails will lead you to some of the other sites, such as the ruins of Matildaville. Many of the trails travel along the Potomac and overlook Great Falls and the rushing rapids of Mather Gorge.

Ride Information

Trail Maintenance Hotline:

National Park Service   (703) 759-2915

Cost:

$2.00 entrance fee at the gate

Schedule:

Park is open from 7:00 A.M. to sunset, closed after dark

Maps:

USGS maps: Vienna, VA; Falls Church, VA
ADC map: Northern Virginia road map
National Park Service Official trail map and guide

(continued from page 119)

Great Falls has always been a popular place to visit for locals and world tourists alike. Some have come to survey the river's rapids, including George Washington, who formed the Patowmack Company in 1784 to build a series of canals around the falls, and Theodore Roosevelt, who came to Great Falls to hike and ride horses during his presidency. Today, thousands come to enjoy Great Falls as well. But they don't come to build canals, develop towns, make trade, or seek solitude from the presidential office. They come only to hike and ride the Park's great trails and witness the magnificent scenery at Great Falls National Park.

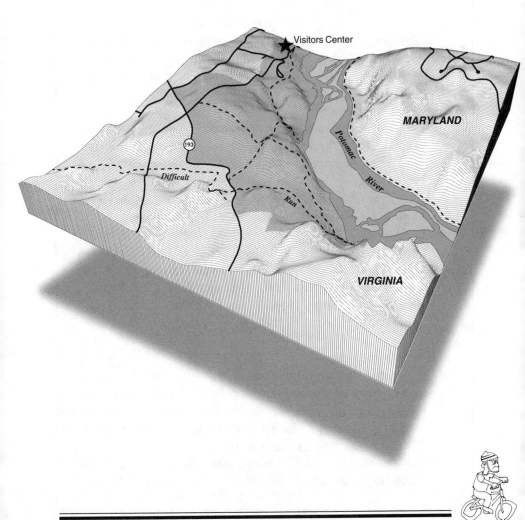

Virginia's
National Forests

The Commonwealth of Virginia is blessed with an abundance of national forest land. Nearly 1.7 million acres of public land was set aside in Virginia in the early 1900s; today forests, lakes, mountain meadows, wildlife, vistas, and scenic wonders await all who wish to explore its endless beauty.

The real treasure of the national forests, however, is that every acre is open to the public. This means that you don't need the landowner's permission to travel on any of the thousands of miles of trails and dirt roads.

In Virginia, there are two national forests that make up the state's huge parcel of public land: the George Washington National Forest and the Jefferson National Forest.

The George Washington National Forest has over one million acres, 945,000 of which are in Virginia. It extends over 140 miles along the Appalachian Mountains in northwestern Virginia and attracts nearly four million visitors per year. Within this forest, there are more than 800 miles of trails open to mountain biking. Endless miles of dirt forest roads connect these trails, which wind up and down the mountain slopes and through the many valleys. In addition, camping is allowed at undeveloped sites almost anywhere within forest boundaries.

The Jefferson National Forest has 690,000 acres of wooded mountains and valleys. It covers much of the state's southwestern portion from the James River south to Mount Rogers. There are over 900 miles of trails and dirt forest roads open to mountain biking.

Located within the Jefferson National Forest is Mount Rogers National Recreation Area. More than 115,000 acres make up this mountainous wonderland, home to Virginia's two highest peaks—Mount Rogers (5,729 feet) and Whitetop Mountain (5,520 feet). There are over 400 miles of trails open to bike travel, all of which wind through the valleys and atop the highest peaks. Mountain biking is welcome throughout the Mount Rogers National

Recreation Area, and because it is within national forest land, camping is allowed at undeveloped sites almost anywhere.

It is important to note that there are some restricted areas and trails within Virginia's national forests that allow only foot and horseback travel. Mountain bikers cannot ride on the Appalachian Trail under any circumstances, and are also restricted from riding in any of the National Forest's Wilderness Areas. None of the rides in this guide use either the Appalachian Trail or Wilderness Areas.

The rides included in *Mountain Bike Virginia* are considered by many cyclists and forest rangers to be some of the more popular places and trails on which to ride in the national forests. While virtually all the trails and forest roads in both the George Washington and Jefferson National Forests are open to everyone, the rides in this guide attempt to avoid routes that might be sensitive to overuse or yield user conflicts. Like all places, however, bicyclists must always yield the right-of-way and tread lightly.

George Washington National Forest

George Washington National Forest HQ	(703) 564-8300
Deerfield Ranger District	(703) 885-8028
Dry River Ranger District	(703) 828-2591
James River Ranger District	(703) 962-2214
Lee Ranger District	(703) 984-4101
Pedlar Ranger District	(703) 261-6105
Warm Springs District	(703) 839-2521

Jefferson National Forest

Jefferson National Forest HQ	(703) 265-6054
Blacksburg Ranger District	(703) 552-4641
Clinch Ranger District	(703) 328-2931
Glenwood Ranger District	(703) 291-2189
New Castle Ranger District	(703) 864-5195
Wythe Ranger District	(703) 228-5551

Mount Rogers National Recreation Area

	(703) 783-5196

15. Elizabeth Furnace

Start: *Opposite campground*	**Terrain:** *Hilly singletrack, forest roads*
Length: *13.3 miles*	**Riding Time:** *3 – 4 hours*
Rating: *Difficult*	**Other Uses:** *Hiking, Horseback*

Climbing to Signal Knob.

L ocated about one hour west of Washington, D.C., just outside Front Royal, Virginia, the tall, northern ridge of Massanutten Mountain stands alone, high above the Shenandoah Valley. Mountain Bikers come in flocks to this northeastern piece of the George Washington National Forest. After cycling its ridge lines and tricky singletrack, it is easy to understand why.

Its proximity to Washington makes it the closest bikeable mountain available to peak-starved Northern Virginia off-roaders. Elizabeth Furnace's many trails travel along and through small creeks, up and down mountain ridges, and to paths where even the most hard-core rock huggers have difficulty keeping their knobby tires grounded. This off-road mountainous sanctuary is not *all* difficult, though. There are plenty of forest roads that travel through the scenic bowl of Fort Valley, a large hollow in between the east and west ridges of Massanutten. (Had he been defeated at the Battle of Yorktown, George Washington would have used this valley as a retreat.) The size of the mountain, the ruggedness of the terrain, and the multitude of terrific cycling trails make the Elizabeth Furnace area an off-road cyclist's dream.

This particular loop takes mountain bikers along a more popular route at Elizabeth Furnace. Some of the terrain on this ride is extremely steep and rugged. The steep sections can be avoided, though, by turning back the same way before committing yourself to a climb. Most of the ride up to the Strasburg Reservoir is only moderately difficult, and if you're not feeling particularly adventurous, just turn around and follow the trails back to the start.

The ride starts from the gravel parking lot off Fort Valley Road and progresses rather easily along Forest Route 1350. Past the gates, the forest road becomes overgrown, rolling up and down the ridge line as it makes its way over Green Mountain. There are some wonderful views of Fort Valley and Massanutten Mountain from this road. Approximately three miles later, FR 1350 ends in what resembles a large, dirt cul-de-sac overrun with small pine trees and tall grass.

You will notice a worn trail descending into the woods at the end of this cul-de-sac. This trail takes you to Little Passage Creek. Take this trail downhill, then turn right and follow the creek (you will cross through the creek five times, so be prepared to get wet) to Massanutten Mountain Road. This road leads to Strasburg Reservoir, which is a good spot to turn around if you would prefer to avoid steep, rocky ascents. For those with a conquering spirit, though, I would recommend making the effort to reach Signal Knob.

Signal Knob's 2,106-foot peak reveals a sweeping panoramic view of the Shenandoah Valley. During the Civil War, Confederate soldiers used the peak to spot Union troops moving south from Winchester. Soldiers hiked what is now the orange-blazed Massanutten Mountain West Trail and searched the valleys below for troop movement. Any information was subsequently flagged from Signal Knob to points farther south. This information would eventually reach the Confederate capital of Richmond.

Most of the Massanutten Mountain West Trail is challenging but quite rideable. Not until the climb's final 500 feet does cycling seem unrealistic and walking becomes the only alternative. The view alone is worth the effort.

The return trip is another story. Grip your brakes and hang low over your rear wheel in order to conquer this double-black-diamond descent. It's quite possible to ride this

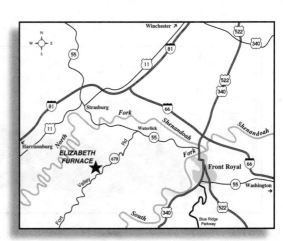

(continued on page 133)

Elizabeth Furnace

☞   **From Front Royal** – Cross the Shenandoah River and follow **VA Route 55** approximately 5 miles west to **Waterlick**. At Waterlick, turn left on **Fort Valley Road (Route 678)** southwest and go 4.5 miles to the gravel parking area on the right, opposite the overnight campground. Turn **right** into the **gravel parking area**. Park here.

MILES   DIRECTIONS

0.0   **START** from the **gravel parking lot** opposite the Elizabeth Furnace overnight campground. Ride west through the **first gate** out of the parking lot and follow **FR (Forest Road) 1350** to the right.

0.1   Go through the **second gate**, continuing up **FR 1350**.

0.2   Pass the Bear Wallow Trail trailhead on the right. Continue on **FR 1350**.

1.4   Reach the end of the first steady climb. FR 1350 starts to roll along Green Mountain. You can see across Fort Valley from this road to the eastern ridge of Massanutten Mountain. This old wagon trail was used extensively back in the 1840s to transport pig iron to Elizabeth Furnace. Fall colors are brilliant along this route.

2.6   Begin a fun descent toward Mudhole Gap.

3.3   FR 1350 ends in what resembles a large, dirt cul-de-sac

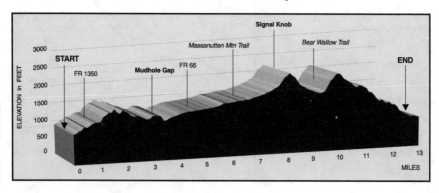

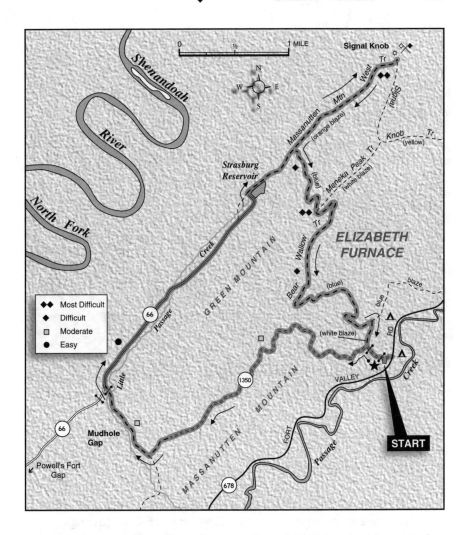

overgrown with small pine and scrub. At the opposite end of this open area is a small trail leading into the woods. Take this short, rocky trail downhill to Little Passage Creek.

3.35   Bear **right** along the creek, traveling upstream through **Mudhole Gap**. Stay on the trail, running parallel with Little Passage Creek. *There are five stream crossings along this trail.*

3.6   First stream crossing.

3.65   Second stream crossing.

Hardcore.

3.8   Third stream crossing.

3.9   Fourth stream crossing.

4.1   Fifth stream crossing. Go around the gate after this last stream crossing, then turn **right** on the **FR 66 (orange blaze)**. This well maintained dirt road heads north toward Strasburg Reservoir and Signal Knob.

6.1   Pass a trailhead on the left. This narrow singletrack trail is an alternate route to Strasburg Reservoir. Both FR 66 and this wet, slightly overgrown trail meet again on the west bank of the reservoir.

Follow FR 66

6.3   Reach the **Strasburg Reservoir**. Turn **left** and **cross the dam**.

6.4 At the other side of the dam, bear **right** with the shoreline. Go another 20 yards to what appears to be the end of the trail at an embankment. Hop over a large rock, push the bike up the embankment, and you should find yourself on the **MASSANUTTEN MOUNTAIN WEST TRAIL (orange blaze)**. This is also the connecting point with the singletrack trail mentioned earlier.

7.0 Pass Bear Wallow Trail (blue blaze) on the right. From this point up to Signal Knob things get pretty steep and difficult.

8.1 Trail goes vertical! The trail becomes little more than a rock slide, as you scale up to the top of the mountain toward Signal Knob. If you can, push yourself to the top. Signal Knob is well worth this extra effort.

8.3 Reach Signal Knob (2,106 feet). Whew! Catch a sweeping view of the Shenandoah Valley. The town of Strasburg is down on the left. Return back down **MASSANUTTEN MOUNTAIN WEST TRAIL** toward Bear Wallow Trail.

8.5 Steep, rocky section ends. Trail becomes a more negotiable singletrack.

9.6 Turn **left** on **BEAR WALLOW TRAIL (blue blaze)**. Begin a grueling, switchback climb to the top of Green Mountain.

10.3 Reach the top of **Green Mountain**. To the left is Meneka Peak Trail (white blaze). Start the descent back down to Elizabeth Furnace, continuing on **BEAR WALLOW TRAIL (blue blaze)**.

10.7 Overlook to Fort Valley.

12.1 Pass the Glass House Trail on the right. Continue **straight** on **BEAR WALLOW TRAIL (blue blaze)**.

12.9 Reach the bottom of a wild descent at the intersection with the blue and white-blazed trails. Turn **right**, following the **WHITE-BLAZED TRAIL** back to FR 1350. The blue-blazed trail travels left across a small creek to Elizabeth Furnace picnic grounds.

13.1   Turn **left** on **FR 1350**, heading back to the car.

13.2   Go around the gate.

13.3   Arrive at the parking lot. Hope you survived the climb over Green Mountain.

Ride Information

Trail Maintenance Hotline:

Lee Ranger District, GW Ntl. Forest	(703) 984-4101
George Washington Ntl. Forest HQ	(703) 564-8300

Schedule:

Public land, accessible year-round

Maps:

USGS maps:	Strasburg, VA; Toms Brook, VA
DeLorme:	VA Atlas & Gazetteer – Page 74 A–2

GW National Forest topo map – Lee Ranger District

National Forest Service trail map

trail down, but be fairly warned of possible misfortune. Luckily, you still have one more chance of returning the easy way before spending the next hour in a singletrack strap—simply return the way you came and avoid most hills. If you choose to continue along this loop, then watch for trail signs on the way down from Signal Knob that direct you to the blue-blazed Bear Wallow Trail. The rewards for cycling Bear Wallow Trail are enormous once on top of Meneka Peak, but these rewards must

be earned. After crossing over a small creek, Bear Wallow heads straight toward the sky over rocks, roots, and ridges. Over the top, the woods become dense and dark where larger trees grow thick, and swallow up the light. Despite its foreboding appearance, the trail repays your strident efforts with an exhilarating, downhill ball-hooter all the way back to the car.

Be prepared to spend anywhere from two to five hours on these trails, so bring plenty of food and water. Tools may also be necessary baggage, considering the nature of some of these trails. Ride hard and have fun!

16. Massanutten Mountain

Start: *Steel gate on Rte 636*	**Terrain:** *Rolling gravel forest roads*
Length: *30 miles*	**Riding Time:** *2 – 3 hours*
Rating: *Moderate*	**Other Uses:** *Automobiles (very light)*

Massanutten Mountain is probably best known for its year-round vacation resort, 18-hole PGA golf course, and 68 acres of downhill skiing. Nonetheless, this private resort area, located 15 minutes east of Harrisonburg, encompasses only the southern tip of this unique mountain, which stretches along the Shenandoah Valley from Harrisonburg all the way to Front Royal. The remaining land on Massanutten is contained within the boundaries of the George Washington National Forest. What this means to cyclists is that more than 90 percent of Massanutten Mountain is open to mountain biking.

Massanutten Mountain is part of the 182,000-acre Lee Ranger District of the George Washington National Forest. The mountain covers roughly one-third of that land and stands apart from the rest of the national forest in the center of the Shenandoah Valley. Bordering Massanutten on the east are the Shenandoah National Park and the Blue Ridge Mountains; the Allegheny Mountains lie to the west. Massanutten's isolated setting within the Shenandoah Valley, its proximity to Harrisonburg, and its unique plow-headed shape make it a landmark for all who travel through Virginia's heartland.

In the late 1800s and early 1900s much of Massanutten Mountain was being mined for iron ore. During that time most of the mountain's southern half was stripped bare of its trees. Later, during the mountain's recovery, a forestry official declared he could not find a single tree more than six inches in diameter.

Since that time, the mountain has managed to recover quite handsomely, with thick forests now covering its craggy slopes. The legacy left by those mining operations is a myriad of old dirt roads and trails used to transport iron ore and other supplies to the many different iron furnaces, including Catherine Furnace and Elizabeth Furnace. These roads and trails are now owned and maintained by the National Forest Service for public use.

This relatively easy ride

Massanutten Mountain rises above the Shenandoah Valley.

starts from the southern end of Massanutten Mountain near Harrisonburg and travels north through its core, revealing the mountain's scenic beauty from a well maintained gravel road. The route starts from the national forest boundary on Route 636. From here, the road becomes gravel and hard-packed dirt.

You will begin with a moderate climb up the mountain through Runkles Gap. The route rolls up and down along Cub Run Road for approximately one mile before descending into the mountain's inner valley along the cascading Cub Run. Just before mile nine, Cub Run intersects with Pitt Spring Run and Roaring Run, both of which turn east and rush downhill before running into the Shenandoah River's south fork. Turn left at this intersection and follow FR 375 uphill along the beautiful Pitt Spring Run (toward the radio towers).

The climb is a workout, but the scenic waterfalls and mountain cliffs provide a wonderful distraction along this route. Don't expect much of an overlook, though, once you reach the radio towers. However, if you peer through the trees you can see to the west over the great Shenandoah Valley and the town of Timberville. To the east, Page Valley and the South Fork Shenandoah River are

(continued on page 139)

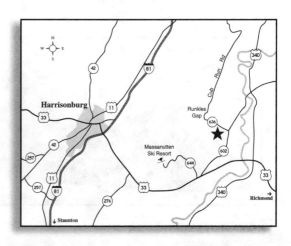

Massanutten Mountain

☞   **From Harrisonburg** – Take **U.S. Route 33 east** for 11 miles toward Massanutten Mountain. Immediately past the entrance for the resort, turn **left** on **Route 602**. Take this approximately 5 miles to Greenwood. At **Greenwood**, turn **left** on **Cub Run Road (Route 636)** and follow this 2 miles up **Massanutten Mountain** into George Washington National Forest. Start at the **George Washington National Forest boundary**, where pavement changes to gravel.

MILES   DIRECTIONS

0.0   **START** on **Route 636** at the **George Washington National Forest boundary**. Park your car on the side of the road and head up the east side of Massanutten Mountain on **CUB RUN ROAD (Route 636)**.

0.1   Go through the gate. Cub Run Road turns to gravel. Begin climbing up Massanutten Mountain's east slope.

0.8   Pass through **Runkles Gap**.

2.3   Reach the top of the first climb (2,152 feet).

7.7   Pass a campground on the right.

9.2   Reach the intersection of Cub Run Road and FR 375. Turn **left** on **FR 375**. Follow along Pitt Spring Run's cascading falls and mountainous scenery.

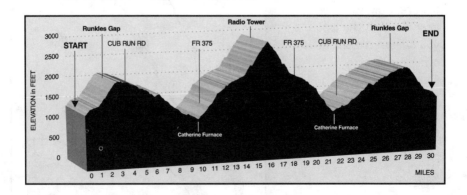

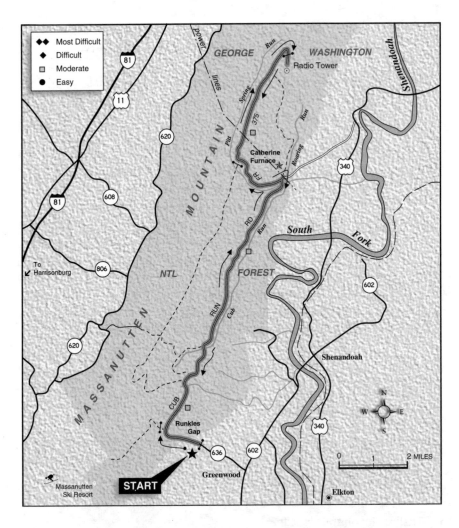

(Note: At this intersection, complete with stop sign, go **straight for 0.25 miles** to reach **Catherine Furnace**. This is one of the old iron furnaces used in the late 1800s to convert iron ore mined on Massanutten Mountain into usable plate iron. The furnace still stands, acting as a monument to times past.)

14.5   Reach the gate just before the radio towers. Go around this gate and continue up the mountain to the summit.

15.0   Reach the summit of **Big Mountain** (one of the peaks of Massanutten Mountain) at 2,962 feet. From this high point you can peak through the trees and see parts of the

Shenandoah Valley to the west and Page Valley to the east. The radio tower is owned and operated by WSVA–TV.

From the summit, turn around, enjoy the descent to Catherine Furnace, and return to the start of the ride the same way you came.

★ Another good place for off-road cycling during certain times of the year is at Massanutten Mountain Resort on the southern tip of the mountain. The resort, which includes the ski slopes and lodging, is privately owned and can't be used without permission. During the summer months, though, when it's too warm for skiing, the resort will often open its wooded trails for hiking and mountain biking. Call the resort for more information about mountain biking and ask for a schedule on trail use. Also, turn to the *Other Rides* section on page 236 for more information regarding mountain biking at area ski resorts.

Ride Information

Trail Maintenance Hotline:

> Lee Ranger District, GW Ntl. Forest   (703) 984-4101
> George Washington Ntl. Forest HQ   (703) 564-8300

Schedule:

> Public land, accessible year-round

Maps:

> USGS maps: Elkton West, VA; Tenth Legion, VA
> DeLorme: VA Atlas & Gazetteer – Page 67 A-6
> GW National Forest topo map – Lee Ranger District

(continued from page 135)

also visible.

The difficulty of this ride is minimal, which, for cyclists wanting a peaceful ride far removed from the motorized world, is just the thing for a quiet and scenic afternoon. To further augment this leisurely ride, bring a lunch and relax along the cascades of Cub Run at one of the many small picnic and parking areas.

Note the trails west of Cub Run Road that seem to parallel Cub Run Road all the way to

FR 375.
These do exist, it's
just a matter of locating them.
And because they fall within the boundaries of
the George Washington National Forest, they are open to off-road cycling should you get anxious for some singletrack while pedaling along the gravel roads. Look for them while on this scenic ride and note the trailheads for the next time. If you choose to try them out, plan on some fairly difficult terrain, so plan ahead with the proper gear.

17. Reddish Knob

Start: *Briery Branch Dam*	**Terrain:** *Mountainous singletrack,road*
Length: *20.5 miles*	**Riding Time:** *2½ – 3 hours*
Rating: *Difficult*	**Other Uses:** *Hiking, hang gliding*

One of the guys at Cool Breeze Cyclery & Fitness in Harrisonburg expounded on a backwoods mountain bike adventure he took with some fellow cyclists into the George Washington National Forest, just west of town. After more than eight hours of cycling virtually endless unexplored trails, he explained, they chose to end their trek because the sheer magnitude of rideable terrain in the mountains and forest land of Augusta County and the Harrisonburg area was just too much for one day. That was all I needed to hear. I pulled my bike from the Yakima rack, eyed the tall mountains to the west, and set out to explore this land of mystic mountain bike terrain.

Augusta County was founded in 1736 and, at its greatest size, embraced land as far west as the Mississippi River. What is now West Virginia, Kentucky, Ohio, Indiana, Illinois, Michigan, Wisconsin, and much of western Pennsylvania was once part of Augusta County. So that frontier residents could more easily access America's court of law and system of justice, Virginia's Augusta County Court was placed in what is known today as Pittsburgh, Pennsylvania.

Although Augusta County no longer contains the land it once held more than two centuries ago, it remains Virginia's second-largest county and includes land from the Blue Ridge to the Alleghenies and much of the Shenandoah Valley. With its thousands of acres of national forest land, it is no wonder such singletrack bounty exits within its boundaries.

My first mountain bike ride into Augusta County's backwoods took me skyward through the George Washington National Forest into the Allegheny Mountains of western Virginia. The ride began up an unforgiving climb to the famed Reddish Knob. As the second-highest peak in Augusta County, Reddish Knob measures in at nearly 4,400 feet above sea level, and the climb to the summit (albeit along a paved road to the top) is relentless. But the views this peak

offers are nothing short of spectacular. Locals claim that on the clearest days, it's possible to see into five states. Regardless, this 360-degree panoramic view from the top of Reddish Knob is certainly one of Virginia's greatest treasures.

The ride begins at the Briery Branch Dam along Route 924, west of Harrisonburg. The climb to Briery Branch Gap, a very long, four-mile stretch of pavement, never eases up. If you're lucky, you might find someone kind enough to drive you to the top of Reddish Knob, then pick you up at the bottom an hour later—the descent may take that long!

If you ride to the top, though, be sure to notice the tombstone less than one half-mile from the summit of Route 924 marking the death of Samual Curry. His body was found December 23, 1922, on this very spot, and no explanation has ever been given. My guess, though, is he was trying to ride a steel-framed prototype mountain bike (circa 1922) all the way to the summit of Reddish Knob. The sheer effort of trying to pedal this ungainly mountain bike up the mountain killed him and set back the development of the sport another 60 years!

Just beyond this gravestone, the sight of which may deal you a demoralizing blow up this climb, you will reach Briery Branch Gap. The roads split here and you will need to bear a hard left, continuing up the paved road toward Reddish Knob. Route 85 gives you the first break on this relentless mountain and reveals the height at which you've climbed. Views of the Shenandoah Valley to the east are breathtaking. At one point along Route 85 you will be riding along the

(continues on page 146)

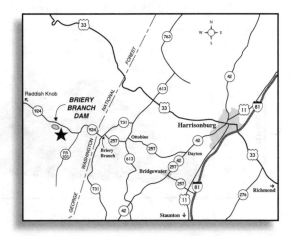

Reddish Knob

☞   **From Harrisonburg** – Take **Route 42 south** for 4½ miles to
Dayton. From Dayton turn **right** on **Route 257** heading **west**. Go
approximately 6 miles to the small town of **Ottobine**. Bear **left**, continuing on **Route 257**. Go 3 miles to **Briery Branch** and turn **left** on **Route
731**. In less than a quarter mile, turn **right** on **Route 924** toward the
mountains. Follow **Route 924** about 5 miles into the George Washington
National Forest to **Briery Branch Dam** on the left. Park here.

MILES   DIRECTIONS

0.0   **START** from the parking area next to **Briery Branch Dam** on
       ROUTE 924 (paved).

0.1   Outdoor toilet on the left.

4.2   Pass Samual Curry's tombstone on the left.

4.4   Reach **Briery Branch Gap**. Turn **hard left**, continuing up the
       mountain on **ROUTE 85** (paved) toward Reddish Knob.

4.6   Cross into Augusta County.

5.5   Overlook on the left.

6.3   The road divides **Virginia** and **West Virginia** along this ridge.
       The ridge is only as wide as the road itself!

6.5   Bear **left** at the split in the road. Continue uphill toward

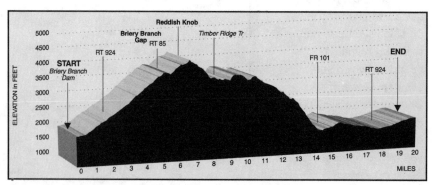

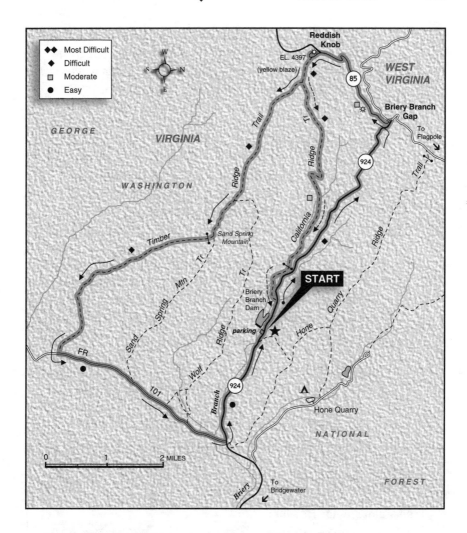

Reddish Knob.

6.9   Reach the summit of **Reddish Knob**!

★ *Return down the road from Reddish Knob to locate Timber Ridge trailhead on the right.*

7.1   Returning downhill from Reddish Knob, turn **right** on **TIMBER RIDGE TRAIL (yellow blaze)**.

*(Note: This trailhead is slightly hidden. Look on the right side of the road for the **large tree with a Budweiser can** nailed to*

*its trunk. Immediately past this tree is a **yellow-diamond marker** on a wooden trail post. This trail starts out a bit sketchy, then crosses a small rock slide. Once past the rock slide, follow the power lines downhill to the trail split.)*

7.4   Cross the rock slide. Vista overlooking Middle Ridge and Buck Mountain on the right.

★ 7.6   Reach the trail split. A wooden trail sign points left to **California Ridge Trail** or right to **Timber Ridge Trail**. Turn **right** on TIMBER RIDGE TRAIL **(yellow blaze)** and continue following the **yellow diamonds** toward Tillman Road (FR 101).

   ★ *(Note: If you're not interested in the long, rugged descent down Timber Ridge, turn left here and follow **California Ridge Trail** back to Briery Branch Dam. California Ridge Trail has a smoother surface and easier terrain. Refer ahead to the California Ridge Trail directions.)*

10.0   **Pass** Wolf Ridge Trail on the left. It is five miles to Tillman Road (FR 101) along Wolf Ridge Trail. Continue **straight**.

10.7   Reach Sandspring Mountain. Bear **right** at this split, continu-

Ride Information

Trail Maintenance Hotline:

   Lee Ranger District, GW Ntl. Forest   *(703) 984-4101*
   George Washington Ntl. Forest HQ   *(703) 564-8300*

Schedule:

   Public land, accessible year-round

Maps:

   USGS maps: Briery Branch, VA; Reddish Knob, VA, WV
   DeLorme: VA Atlas & Gazetteer – Page 66 A-2
   GW National Forest topo map – Lee Ranger District

ing to follow
**TIMBER RIDGE
TRAIL (yellow
blaze)**. Watch
out for the
steel bar
across Timber
Ridge Trail
fewer than 20
yards from
this split.

Cyclists make time for a photo op' on the summit of Reddish Knob.

14.7   Reach the bottom of one of the best descents on the planet!
Turn **left** on **TILLMAN ROAD (FR 101)**, a well-maintained gravel
road, which is nearly all downhill to Route 924.

18.3   Turn **left** on **ROUTE 924** (paved), back to **Briery Branch Dam**.

20.5   Reach **Briery Branch Dam** and the end of the ride.

★ CALIFORNIA RIDGE TRAIL ★

★ **7.6**   At this trail split, turn **left** on **CALIFORNIA RIDGE TRAIL**.

9.7   Cross Briery Branch. Singletrack changes to a jeep trail.

10.5   Cross Briery Branch again.

11.1   Go around the **steel gate**.

*(Note: You will actually re-enter George Washington National
Forest around this gate. Forest rangers plan to reroute this
section of trail in the near future so it does not cross
through private land. Remember to always follow the yellow-
blazed trail down the ridge.)*

12.5   Trail bears **hard left**, then ends at Route 924. Turn **right** on
ROUTE 924 and pass Briery Branch Reservoir.

12.7   Arrive at the start of the ride.

Views from on top of the world.

(continued from page 141)

Virginia-West Virginia state line. Pedaling on the left side of the road takes you into Virginia; the right leads to West Virginia. A few more pedal strokes and you reach Reddish Knob.

Finding the trailhead to the Timber Ridge and California Ridge trails can be tricky. If you're traveling downhill from Reddish Knob you will pass a large tree on the right with a Budweiser can nailed to the trunk. A slightly hidden, wooden post with a yellow-diamond marker shows the trail on the right just past this tree. Thus begins your wild descent.

Near the beginning of this trail, you will have to cross a small rock slide before descending to the main split. A large wooden sign will direct you left or right to either California Ridge Trail or Timber Ridge Trail. These two trails are dramatically different from one another, but equally fun.

California Ridge Trail is a shorter and much smoother singletrack that descends along a well-worn trail through thick mountain laurel. As it nears the end, the trail widens into a jeep road along Briery Branch. If you're running short on time or looking for something less technical but still challenging, then take this fun route back to the dam. If your cycling aspirations run higher, turn right at the trail split and follow Timber Ridge Trail.

Timber Ridge Trail does not immediately run downhill as does the California Ridge Trail. You must negotiate a number of rolling hills along the rocky ridge before being rewarded with an extraordinary descent. Then, at the point where Timber Ridge Trail turns right from Sand Springs Mountain, the trail drops altitude quickly and sends you flying down a wooded trail for more than four miles. Watch out for hazards as you near the bottom—the descent is like no other and may send you airborne at any instant.

FR 101 carries you back to Route 924 on a mostly downhill gravel road. The rest of the ride from here is "cake," allowing you to recount the downhill of a lifetime all the way back to the car.

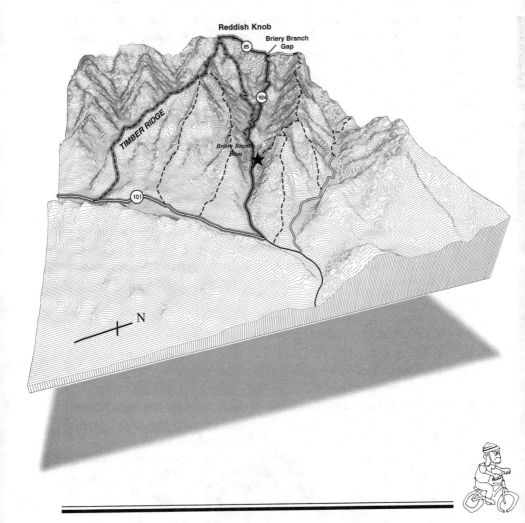

18. Flagpole

Start: *Briery Branch Dam*
Length: *17.6 miles*
Rating: *Difficult*

Terrain: *Mountainous singletrack*
Riding Time: *2½ hours*
Other Uses: *Hiking, Horseback*

This ride is one of the state's all-time greats. Its only drawback, perhaps, is the daunting 7½-mile climb in the first 7½ miles of the ride—not much of a warm-up.

Again, like the ride up to Reddish Knob, start from the parking area at Briery Branch Dam before climbing the relentless ascent up Route 924 to Briery Branch Gap. Once you reach the Gap, rather than turning left toward Reddish Knob, continue straight, following the hard, rocky dirt road. This road quickly switches north along the top of the Shenandoah Mountain's ridgeline and travels parallel to the Virginia-West Virginia border. There is another 3½ miles of climbing before reaching Flagpole.

It hardly seems reasonable to spend the first 7½ miles climbing. But like those long chair lift rides to the top of the nation's greatest downhill ski runs, you will reach the summit, take a deep breath, and launch yourself on an incredible journey to the bottom.

And what a journey this ride becomes! At mile 7.8, bear right, off the main road, through a hollow of trees to reach the grassy, mountaintop meadow called Flagpole. You may notice a pine tree on the edge of this meadow that is much taller than its neighbors. This wind-blown tree distinguishes itself because it can be seen from the roads below, resembling a flag on a flagpole blowing in the strong mountain winds.

The view from Flagpole is spectacular, and on a clear day you can see east over the mountaintops into the Shenandoah Valley. Though the view is less dramatic than that from the summit of Reddish Knob, you will see the popular mountain peak not far to the south.

While enjoying the view from Flagpole, gather your wits and replenish your system, because awaiting you just down the road is the orange-blazed Slate Springs trailhead. Slate Springs Trail is the path that will take you on a crazy downhill adventure.

From Flagpole, get back on the dirt road and ride only one tenth of a mile. Keep a sharp eye on the right side of the road for the

A lone cyclist crosses the meadows atop Flagpole. A lengthy descent begins just over this crest.

bright, orange-diamond trail marker tacked to a tree. This marker is partially hidden, so if you pass a small camping area on the left and go sharply downhill on this main road, then you've gone too far.

For nearly seven long miles after turning onto Slate Springs AA Jeep Trail, you will descend twisting, narrow singletrack that contours the mountain, pass a rocky overlook, then drop vertically down a grassy trail littered with moguls. If you're not careful, the

(continued on page 153)

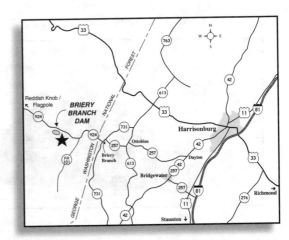

Flagpole

☞   From Harrisonburg – Take **Route 42 south** for 4½ miles to **Dayton**. From Dayton turn **right** on **Route 257** heading **west**. Go about 6 miles and reach the small town of **Ottobine**. Bear **left**, continuing on **Route 257**. Go about 3 miles to **Briery Branch** and turn **left** on **Route 731**. In less than a quarter mile, turn **right** on **Route 924** toward the mountains. Follow **Route 924** about 5 miles into the George Washington National Forest to **Briery Branch Dam** on the left. Park here.

MILES   DIRECTIONS

0.0   **START** from the parking area next to **Briery Branch Dam** on **ROUTE 924** (paved).

0.1   Outdoor toilet on the left.

4.2   Pass Samual Curry's tombstone up the embankment on the left. Might this be foreshadowing the day's ride?

4.4   Reach the intersection at **Briery Branch Gap**. Continue **straight** on the DIRT ROAD, climbing northeast toward Flagpole.

5.4   Pass Hone Quarry Ridge Jeep Trail on the right.

5.5   Overlook on the right. A short trail from the road takes you to this overlook, then brings you back to the **DIRT ROAD**.

7.7   Reach **Flagpole**! Bear **right** to get to the meadow. To continue

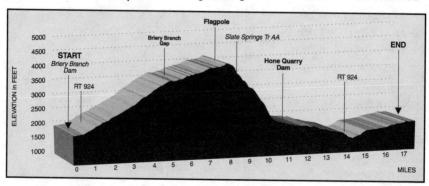

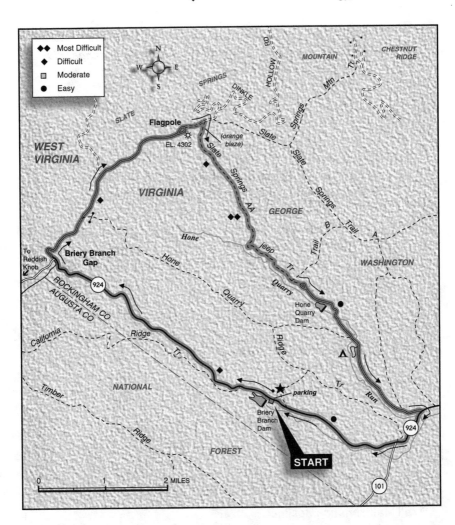

this ride, get back on the **DIRT ROAD** and head northeast.

7.8 Just past Flagpole, turn **right** from the dirt road on **SLATE SPRINGS AA JEEP TRAIL**. This narrow singletrack clings to the edge of the ridge. Your brake pads will be smoking by the end of this descent.

(Note: The trailhead for **Slate Springs AA Jeep Trail** is hidden. On the left, immediately preceding this trailhead, is a small clearing used for primitive camping. There is a stone campfire ring in the clearing. Past this campground, the dirt road drops downhill very dramatically. You've gone too far if *you pass this primitive campground and begin a dramatic, rocky descent. Look on the right for a* **bright, orange, diamond trail marker** *tacked to a tree just below the dirt road.)*

8.7   Rock outcrop overlooking Hone Quarry Ridge. Stop and let your brakes cool. Prepare for a very steep, grassy descent.

10.4   Reach the bottom of the descent and bear to the **right**, continuing on the **orange-blazed trail**. Travel downhill, following along Hone Quarry Creek toward the Reservoir.

10.7   Slate Springs AA Jeep Trail ends at a **dirt road**. Turn **left** on this **DIRT ROAD**. Notice the metal trailpost marking the trail you were just on. There is a picture of a horse, hiker, and **mountain biker** on it.

11.1   Pass Hone Quarry Reservoir on the right.

14.9   Turn **right** on **ROUTE 924** (paved).

17.6   Reach **Briery Branch Dam**.

Ride Information

Trail Maintenance Hotline:

Lee Ranger District, GW Ntl. Forest   (703) 984-4101

George Washington Ntl. Forest HQ   (703) 564-8300

Schedule:

Public land, accessible year-round

Maps:

USGS maps: Briery Branch, VA; Brandywine, W.VA, VA

DeLorme: VA Atlas & Gazetteer — Page 66 A-2

GW National Forest topo map — Lee Ranger District

(continued from page 149)

moguls may launch you into the air. The trail at the bottom of this descent becomes so steep that those of you with two-fingered brake levers will be braking with everything you can by the end. The descent finally tapers off and follows the orange blazes across Hone Quarry Run, then along a fast, dirt road toward Route 924. Pass the Hone Quarry Reservoir, glide through a tunnel of tall pines, then coast up to the paved road (Route 924). Turn right on this road and pedal back to the start of the ride.

If we could only get to the top in a gondola, we could do that ride over and over again.

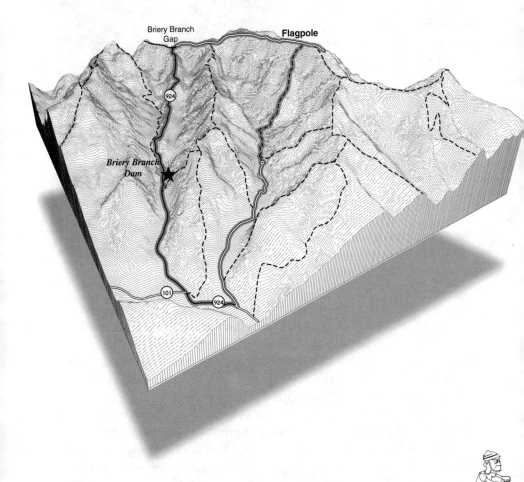

19. Ellis Loop Trail

Start: *Dun's Gap Rd parking*	**Terrain:** *Dirt roads, singletrack*
Length: *5.6 miles*	**Riding Time:** *1 hour*
Rating: *Moderate*	**Other Uses:** *Hiking, Horseback*

In this land of bubbling, high-mountain spas, where hot springs well up from the earth at an average temperature of 104 degrees, where diplomats, presidents, world travelers, and tired Virginians come to rejuvenate their weary bodies, and where the luxurious Homestead Resort has resided for more than two centuries, a new kind of recreation is taking shape. Near Hot Springs, Virginia, in the hills of the Allegheny Mountains, lie hundreds of miles of open mountain biking trails.

The Homestead.

Mountain bikers throughout the region are making tracks to the Warm Springs Valley of Virginia's western slopes. They come to explore the off-road avenues of picturesque hillsides and pleasant hidden valleys, test their wits on rugged singletrack, or pedal slowly through mountain-rimmed meadows. Then, after trekking exhaustively through the backcountry, these active vacationers can visit one of the area's many hot mineral spas and "take the cure," soaking their tired bodies in naturally heated springs. Does it get any better than this? Well, sure, if you never leave.

There are plenty of places to stay in the Warm Springs Valley. The region has several campgrounds, and primitive camping in the George Washington National Forest is virtually limitless. But why bother sleeping under the stars after a long ride when you can stay where the stars sleep? The Homestead, Virginia's premier

Follow this jeep road toward Warm Springs Mountain.

resort, pulls out all the stops for weary travelers, and makes a visit to the Warm Springs Valley a world-class event. For cyclists staying at the resort, The Homestead now offers off-road guided tours and rents bikes from the ski lodge.

As for the ride itself, this exciting five-mile loop is close enough to Hot Springs to pedal from the resort to the ride's start (less than four miles). Get on Route 220 and head north toward Mitchelltown. After little over one mile, bear left up a narrow, paved road (the only left turn before Mitchelltown); this is Route 618. Follow Route 618 uphill for one mile to a gate, where Dun's Gap Road (Route 618) turns left and changes to dirt. Follow this another one and a

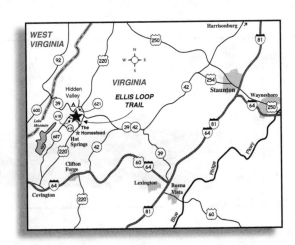

(continued on page 158)

Ellis Loop Trail

☞   **From Hot Springs** – Take **U.S. 220 north** for approximately 1½ miles. Immediately before Mitchelltown, turn **left** on **Route 618**. Follow this uphill for nearly 2 miles to a gate. Pavement ends. Bear **left**, continuing on **Route 618 (Dun's Gap Road)**. This is now a dirt road. Follow **Dun's Gap Road** a little more than 2 miles along Cowardin Run. There is a **small, gravel parking area** on the left. Park here. The ride starts to the right on Dun's Gap Road.

MILES   DIRECTIONS

0.0   **START** at the **parking area** on Dun's Gap Road (Route 618). Turn **right** on DUN'S GAP ROAD.

0.05   Turn **hard left** through the gate on the **DIRT JEEP ROAD**. This dirt road carries you uphill for a spectacular view of the surrounding area.

0.3   Reach the top of this climb.

1.0   Great view to the left of the distant mountains. This is a very leisurely, scenic road through this valley.

2.1   Reach the bottom of a fun descent. Turn **left** on **ELLIS TRAIL**. You've gone too far if you cross the stream at the bottom of this descent.

(Note: Ellis Trail is marked with a **black, wooden arrow** tacked

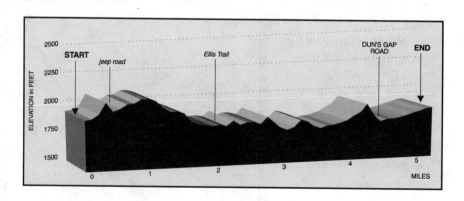

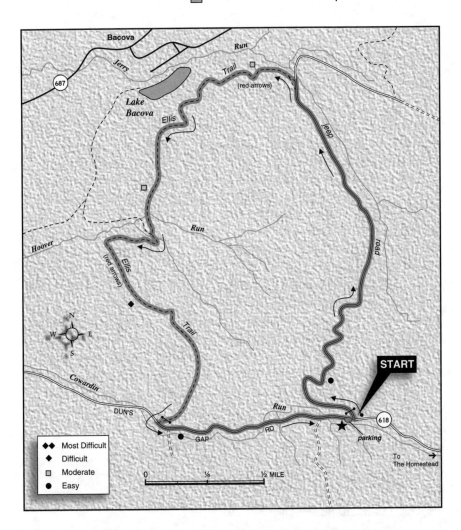

*to a tree. This arrow, **marked #20**, points into the woods. Once in the woods, Ellis Trail is marked with **large, wooden, red arrows**.)*

2.7   **Lake Bacova** is visible through the trees on the right.

4.9   Go down a very steep descent, through a gate, then turn **left** on **DUN'S GAP ROAD**. Follow **DUN'S GAP ROAD** upstream with **Cowardin Run** to the parking area.

5.6   Reach the parking area.

(continued from page 155)

half miles along Cowardin Run to the start of the ride. Parking is available if you choose to drive.

Ellis Loop Trail starts at a small, gravel parking area on Route 618. From here, turn right on 618, traveling fewer than 20 yards, then turn hard left through a gate and ride uphill on an old jeep road. Look for the wonderful view of the Warm Springs Mountain at the top of this climb. This jeep road winds through a little valley along mostly flat terrain until a swift descent carries you down toward Jerry Run. Be sure to keep your eyes peeled for a black, wooden arrow that points left into the woods (the trailhead for Ellis Trail). You've gone too far if you cross a creek along the jeep road. Once you locate the trailhead, notice that Ellis Trail is marked with large, wooden, red arrows all the way to Dun's Gap Road (Route 618).

Because Ellis Trail is a multiple-use trail, you will probably notice lots of horse tracks and possibly some ATV tracks. Chances are, though, you will be alone in this secluded wilderness as you roll along a trail that, at times, should challenge even experienced riders. Just before Ellis Trail ends, there is one last steep climb precluding a very fast descent to the road. Be careful on this descent—there's a gate at the bottom that is usually closed and can catch you off-guard. Be careful not to run into it!

Ride Information

Trail Maintenance Hotline:

Warm Springs Ranger District	(703) 839-2521
George Washington Ntl. Forest HQ	(703) 564-8300
The Homestead	1-800-838-1766
	(703) 839-1766

Schedule:

Public land, accessible year-round

Maps:

USGS maps:	Warm Springs, VA
DeLorme:	VA Atlas & Gazetteer – Page 64 D-4

GW National Forest topo map – Warm Springs District

   Turn left on Dun's Gap Road (Route 618), and head back along
Cowardin Run toward the start of the ride. The soothing sounds of
Cowardin Run's cascading water may remind you of the hot mineral
baths awaiting you back at the resort.

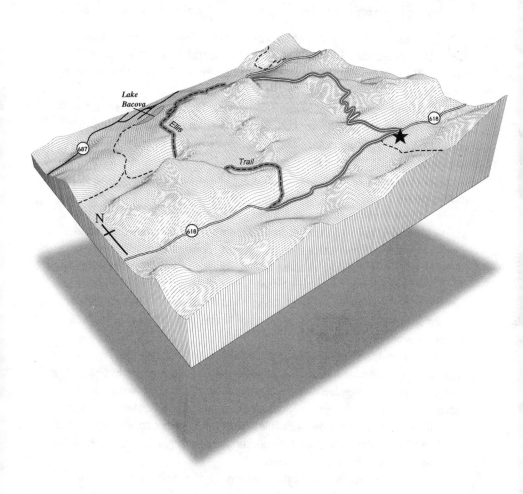

20. Hidden Valley

Start: *Past campgrounds on 241* **Terrain:** *Jeep trails, singletrack, dirt roads*

Length: *11 miles* **Riding Time:** *1½ – 2 hours*

Rating: *Moderate* **Other Uses:** *Hiking, Horseback*

Deep in the Allegheny Mountains of western Virginia there is a quiet little place called Hidden Valley. This peaceful hollow is situated just west of Warm Springs, cradled within the green mountains of the George Washington National Forest.

Warm Springs is renowned for the natural hot springs that well up from deep below the ground on which the town is built. As you drive through Warm Springs notice the large, white spring boxes containing the relaxing and therapeutic mineral baths. Perhaps this is just the thing you will need after an arduous mountain bike ride in the hills of the nearby mountains.

If you have the time and money, reserve a night at The Homestead and spend a wonderful evening whining and dining at this world-class resort. The Homestead Resort in Hot Springs is fewer than six miles from the secluded pastures and farmland of Hidden Valley. Hit the trails for an early-morning ride, treat yourself to a five-course lunch and mineral bath back at the resort, then head back to the mountains to explore some of the hundreds of miles of trails and dirt roads that crisscross the area.

The Hidden Valley Loop starts at the end of the road beyond the Hidden Valley Campgrounds. Just across the Jackson River is the historic Warwick Mansion, which was the site of the recent motion picture *Sommersby*, starring Richard Gere and Jodie Foster. Some of the buildings from the movie set are still there. The restored mansion is now the Hidden Valley Bed and Breakfast, which may serve you well if The Homestead doesn't fit your budget.

The loop travels along flat terrain for the first half of the ride and parallels the clear waters of the Jackson River. There are three occasions in which you must cross the river to continue on the old jeep road. Only once, however, do you have   the option of crossing over the river (the first crossing can be   made walking across the swinging bridge. Just before   the trail leads you to FR 241, you must ford the river   twice more with your bike over your   shoulder. The water

Hidden Valley.

is only knee deep and the currents aren't too strong, but be careful during the rainy seasons. The river can swell its banks, becoming too dangerous to cross by foot. Keep this in mind before planning your ride.

After crossing the river for the third and final time, you will follow a jeep road through a thick grove of pines to a well maintained gravel road with a choice of directions. To continue the Hidden Valley Loop, you must take a hard left off the gravel road around a metal gate. This leads you onto an overgrown dirt road that goes up a short incline (FR 241 west). The road's appearance improves dramatically as soon as you crest this small hill. From here, follow this rolling dirt road all the way back to Hidden Valley. You will pass the entrance to the Hidden Valley Bed and Breakfast on your way down the last hill on FR 241, then cross over the Jackson River before arriving back at the start of the loop. Consider cycling over to the Warwick Mansion and pedaling through the *Sommersby* movie set before leaving this beautiful valley.

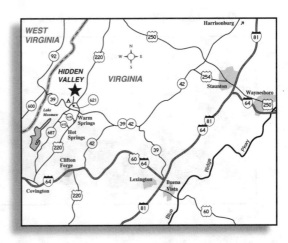

Hidden Valley

☞   **From Hot Springs** – Take **U.S. 220 north** approximately 15 miles to **Warm Springs** and turn **left** on **Route 39 west**. Follow **Route 39 west** approximately 10 miles and turn **right** on **Route 621** to the **Hidden Valley Campgrounds**. Route 621 splits in 3 miles. Bear **left**, following **Route 241**. Pass Hidden Valley Campgrounds in 5 miles. Route 241 turns to dirt. Go another 1½ miles past the campground until it dead-ends at the **cul-de-sac**. There is a portable toilet here. The trail starts from the steel gate on the right.

MILES   DIRECTIONS

0.0   **START** at the **cul-de-sac** on **Route 241** beyond the Hidden Valley Campground. Go through the steel gate (marked "road closed") on the east side of this parking area and follow the **HIDDEN VALLEY TRAIL** along the wagon track through the fields of Poor Farm.

0.1   Pass a tree with a **brown arrow** directing you north along the Jackson River through Poor Farm.

0.5   Pass another **brown arrow** directing you away from the Jackson River to the middle of Poor Farm. Follow the wagon trail across the field.

0.6   Pass beneath a grove of trees and an overgrown, wooden gateway. The trail continues straight through the field.

0.9   Leave the open fields of Poor Farm and enter into the thick

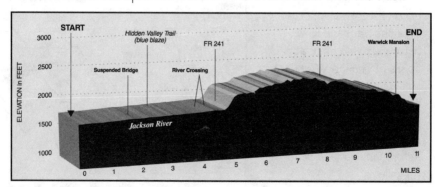

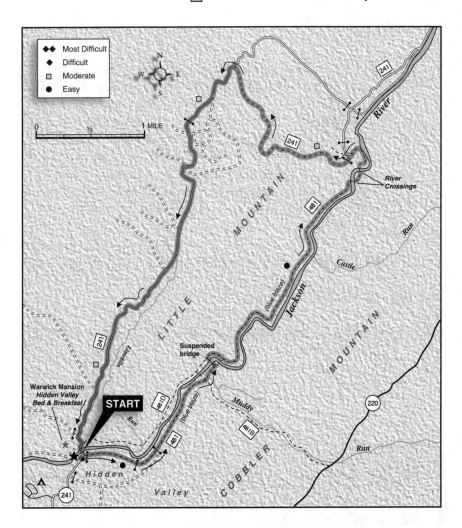

woods on a flat jeep road **(FR 481)** paralleling the Jackson River. Two wooden posts mark the entrance. This section of the **HIDDEN VALLEY TRAIL** is **blue-blazed**.

1.5 There is a trail sign on the left of the jeep road. Turn **left** at this sign following the **HIDDEN VALLEY TRAIL—FR 481 (blue blaze)**. Cross over a little wooden foot bridge toward Jackson River. If you were to continue bearing right on what appears to be the main trail, you would end up on **Muddy Run Trail (481B)**, which takes you to Route 220.

1.6 Reach the swinging bridge that spans across the **Jackson**

River.

*(Note: If you would prefer to stay dry, then cross over the Jackson River via the swinging bridge. Once across the bridge, turn **right** on a little grassy foot trail that scales the hillside above the river. Follow this overgrown path down toward the river. This little trail leads you to the same spot on the blue-blazed Hidden Valley Trail (FR 481) that you would be had you waded across the river. Choosing the bridge route keeps you dry—but only for now. You still must cross the river twice more, and there are no more bridges. Plan to get wet. From here, **FR 481** continues along the left side of Jackson River.)*

3.4   **FR 481** becomes a grassy doubletrack. Cross a small stream.

3.6   **FR 481** changes back to a jeep road.

3.8   Cross the **Jackson River**. Time to get wet! The river should be not quite knee deep and about 40-50 feet across. You can see the trail continuing on the other side. Walk carefully, the bottom may be slippery.

3.9   Cross the **Jackson River** again. The river is about knee deep

Ride Information

Trail Maintenance Hotline:

Warm Springs Ranger District	(703) 839-2521
George Washington Ntl. Forest HQ	(703) 564-8300
Hidden Valley Bed & Breakfast	(703) 839-3178
The Homestead	1-800-838-1766

Schedule:

Public land, accessible year-round

Maps:

USGS maps:	Warm Springs, VA; Sunrise, VA, W.VA
DeLorme:	VA Atlas & Gazetteer – Page 64 D-4
GW National Forest topo map – Warm Springs District	

here. Be careful of the slick rocks on the bottom.

4.0 Follow **FR 481** through a small pine forest. Go up a little hill, then around a steel gate. The road now changes to **FR 241**, which takes you all the way back to the start.

4.1 **FR 241** comes to a split. Take a **hard left** around the **steel gate**. Once you reach the top of the small incline, the crushed-stone, shale-surfaced route becomes a very rideable and well maintained forest road.

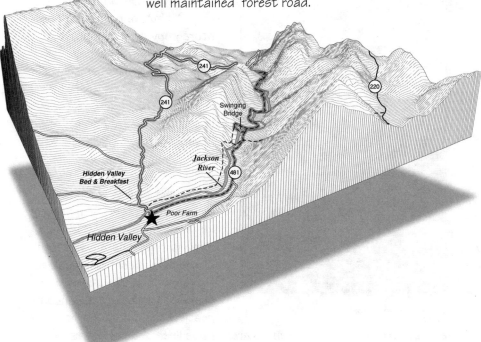

6.7 Go around a gate.

10.3 Go around another gate. It's all downhill to Hidden Valley from this last gate.

10.8 Reach the bottom of a wild descent along **FR 241**. Pass the **Hidden Valley Bed and Breakfast** on the right. Bear left on this road. Cross over the river on a small **concrete bridge**.

11.0 Arrive back at the parking area.

21. Sherando Lake Loop

Start: *Turkey Pen Tr. parking lot* **Terrain:** *Singletrack, dirt/paved roads*
Length: *18.2 miles*   **Riding Time:** *2 – 2½ hours*
Rating: *Moderate to Difficult*   **Other Uses:** *Hiking*

Sherando's upper lake.

A friendly face at Waynesboro's Rockfish Gap Outfitters pointed at the store-copy topo map and revealed, tapping his finger amidst the thick green contour lines, that this was where he sends off-road riders who come in search of alpine adventure. "You want great trails," he said coolly, "you go here."

"Here" turned out to be one of the largest slabs of mountain I had ridden in Central Virginia. These massive levels of ancient orogeny are just south of the magnificent Shenandoah National Park. They tower above the fertile valley of Shenandoah, nestling the riches of this eastern bread basket between its great ridge lines and the slopes of western Virginia's Allegheny Highlands.

I turned into the gravel parking lot off FR 42 and contemplated my ascent into what is commonly known as "Big Levels."

Big Levels has much more to offer than just rugged ridge lines and rocky terrain, though. Between such ominous sounding peaks as Torry Ridge and Devil's Knob lie the peaceful upper and lower lakes of Sherando. Both were built in the early 1900s by the Civilian Conservation Corps for both recreational use and flood control. The lower lake is used for swimming, boating, and fishing; the upper lake is known primarily for its good fishing.

Camping is also popular at Sherando Lake, which has more than 60 units and a large group camping area.

Other nearby scenic wonders include the Blue Ridge Parkway, which rolls along the summits of mountains south of Big Levels; Saint Mary's Wilderness, along the southwest slopes of Big Levels; and the cascades of Saint Mary's Falls.

From the parking lot off FR 42, Turkey Run Trail begins its slow ascent on an old logging road. The trail narrows just beyond one mile into a thick-foliaged singletrack, gaining elevation at such a mild rate you may wonder at times if you're going uphill at all. This changes dramatically, however, at mile 5.5, when the trail lifts off and aims upward to Bald Mountain Overlook. You might not mention to anyone that you needed to push your bike up this section of the trail, but no one will believe you anyway if you say you didn't. The trail is slightly more than handlebar-width with little room for bike handling errors (one side of the trail is a wall of earth, while the other side is an unnerving drop through hundreds of feet of rugged terrain). For some, this poses no challenge, but with more than 1,000 feet of vertical climbing and eight sharp switchbacks in under one mile, the trail becomes a true adventure.

The reward? A few aches in the legs, spectacular views, more than 10 miles of furious downhill (all the way back to the ride's start), and the satisfaction of completing a truly rigorous course.

The descent begins at the top of that climb and winds down a rocky fire road to Bald Mountain Overlook and the Blue Ridge Parkway. Turn left on the Parkway (rarely any traffic to contend with along this well maintained, scenic highway), and let gravity pull you for more than three miles past a number of scenic overlooks. Turn left just before the Parkway starts climbing and continue downward along White Rock Gap Trail (orange blaze) through an old pine forest. This fun singletrack trail glides downhill for more than two miles before depositing you at Sherando's upper lake.

There are restrooms at the different campground areas in

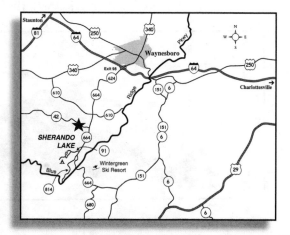

(continued on page 171)

Sherando Lake Loop

☞   From I-64 near Waynesboro – Take **Exit-96** (Waynesboro-Lyndhurst exit). Follow signs to Sherando Lake. Follow **VA 624** 2½ miles to Lyndhurst. At Lyndhurst, bear **left** on **VA 664 south**. Go approximately 5.3 miles on **VA 664**, through Sherando, to FR 42. Turn **right** on **FR 42** (dirt road) and travel a ½ mile to the **first parking area on your left**. This is the **Turkey Pen Trail parking lot**. Park here.

MILES   DIRECTIONS

0.0   **START** at the **Turkey Pen Trail parking lot** off FR 42. **Turkey Pen Trail (blue blaze)** starts from the far left corner of the parking lot.

1.2   **TURKEY PEN TRAIL** narrows into a singletrack trail. Fairly gradual climb. Marked by **blue diamond blazes**.

2.6   Turn **right** and cross the stream. **TURKEY PEN TRAIL** continues on the other side. Look for the **blue blazes**.

5.5   Begin the steep ascent.

5.6   Round the first of nine switchbacks as you scale the slopes of this ridge toward Bald Mountain Overlook.

6.5   At last, reach the summit! The trail exits into a clearing used for primitive camping. Bear right through this clearing, pedaling toward the fire road. Turn **left** on **FR 162 (BALD MOUNTAIN PRIMITIVE ROAD)**. This dirt road carries you east

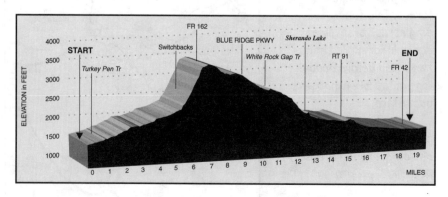

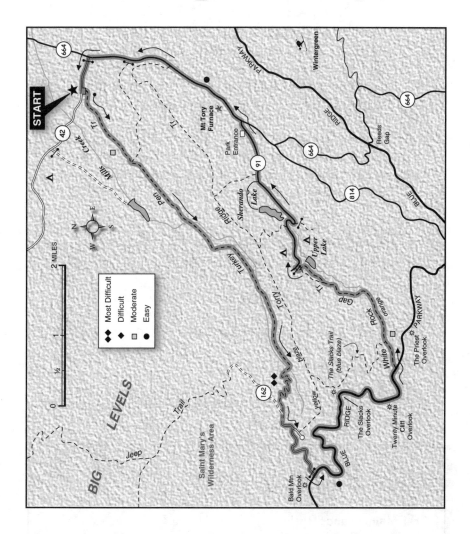

toward the Blue Ridge Parkway and Bald Mountain Overlook.

6.8   Pass the road up to the old fire tower.

★ *Portable toilet at the old fire tower location.*

7.3   Turn **left** on the **BLUE RIDGE PARKWAY**. Bald Mountain
Overlook is on the right. This scenic, paved descent takes you
downhill all the way to White Rock Gap Trail. You've gone too
far if you begin any significant climbs on the Parkway.

10.3   Turn **left** off the Parkway on **WHITE ROCK GAP TRAIL**. This is just before the Parkway starts a significant climb. Keep your eyes peeled for a small clearing to the left. There are often cars parked here. Also near the road, next to this clearing, is an orange diamond tacked to a tree. The trailpost for White Rock Gap Trail is a few feet into the woods.

"The Old Mountain Homesite: Much of the Blue Ridge area was settled in the early 1700s and cleared for agricultural purposes. The land was not economically suited for small farms. These farms were abandoned in the 1860s with the opening of western lands and the Civil War." U.S.F.S.

12.3   Reach Sherando's upper lake and the paved park road. Turn **right** on the **PARK ENTRANCE ROAD (ROUTE 91)**. Follow this downhill past Sherando's lower lake to the park exit.

14.9   Turn **left** on **ROUTE 664**, exiting Sherando Lake Park.

16.3   Pass Mount Torry Furnace on the left.

17.8   Turn **left** on **FR 42**.

18.2   Reach Turkey Pen Trail parking lot and the end of a very long descent!

Ride Information

Trail Maintenance Hotline:

    Pedlar Ranger District   *(703) 261-6105*

    George Washington Ntl. Forest HQ   *(703) 564-8300*

Cost:

    $2.00 per vehicle, $4.00 for parking at the swim site

Schedule:

    Main gate open 6 A.M. to 10 P.M.

Maps:

    USGS maps: Sherando, VA; Big Levels, VA

    DeLorme: VA Atlas & Gaetteer – Page 54 A-3

    GW National Forest topo map – Pedlar Ranger District

(continued from page 167)

the Sherando Lake area and ice and vending machines in the open area at the beach house pavilion near the lower lake. Outside the park (along Route 664, heading back to the start of the ride) there's a general store with food and drinks.

Another point of interest on the way back to the start of the ride is Mount Torry Furnace on Route 664. This old iron furnace was built in 1804 to process iron ore mined in the nearby mountains. It was destroyed in 1864 during the Civil War, then rebuilt and operated until 1884.

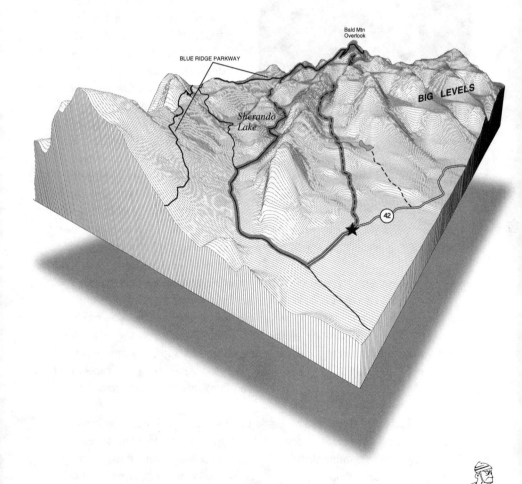

22. Big Levels

Start: *Sherando's Upper Lake*	**Terrain:** *Singletrack, jeep/dirt/paved rds*
Length: *26.8 miles*	**Riding Time:** *4 – 5 hours*
Rating: *Most Difficult*	**Other Uses:** *Hiking, ATV, Automobiles*

Narrow singletrack trails along rocky ridge lines and steep, barren, sun-baked jeep trails characterize this grueling route, one of the most difficult rides in this book. It's important to remember on a ride like this to bring lots of water and food because there aren't any 7-Elevens out in the woods where you can grab a tasty Super Big Gulp. Another suggestion before starting this ride is to invest in some type of front-end suspension. The steep and rocky nature of these trails will probably cause more shock to the body than arms and backs were meant to absorb. Without shocks, you may end this ride quite sore.

The Big Levels ride begins at the Sherando Lake Campground near Sherando's upper lake. To get there, follow the park access road through the park toward the group campgrounds. Immediately after the final turn, before the group camping area, there is a grassy meadow next to the upper lake dam. The White Rock Gap trailhead is on the far side of this meadow at the gate. You may leave your car in the parking area just past the trailhead.

White Rock Gap Trail crosses the meadow and heads into the woods, following small metal orange blazes tacked to the trees. The trail splits almost immediately, heading either straight on the jeep road paralleling the lake or right, climbing into the woods. Either way will deposit you on White Rock Gap Trail, which follows the

Camelbacks are a necessity on tough rides like this.

10.3 Cross a small creek (John's Run).

11.3 The trail becomes very rocky and steep. Follow the **switchback route** rather than the straight route.

14.5 Reach the bottom of this treacherous descent! Go around the gate and turn **right** on **FR 42** (unpaved).

21.8 Turn **right** on **VA 664 (paved)**, heading back to Sherando Lake.

22.4 Convenience store on the right. Ahh, refreshments!

22.8 Mount Torry Furnace on the right.

24.2 Turn **right** into Sherando Lake Park on **ROUTE 91.** Remember to carry your receipt with you so you don't have to worry about paying a second time to get back into the park.

26.1 Pass the lower lake.

26.8 Reach the group campground. Is your body devastated?

(continued from page 173)

and avoid the extremely difficult descent down Big Levels Primitive Road. Kennedy Ridge, however, is still very difficult in its own right.

You will encounter one more intersection along Big Levels Primitive Road (FR 162) before making the descent down Big Levels. Loose dirt and sand make up the surface cover at the spot where you must bear right and begin crisscrossing down the ridge to FR 42. This section down to the bottom can be extremely difficult and will take some time to maneuver. Large rocks, steep grades, and the elements of fatigue combine to make this a true mountain biker's challenge. Be sure not to follow the trail that heads straight down—a straight-line descent does not always mean a faster descent. This deteriorating jeep trail is little more than a two-lane rock slide clear to the bottom of the mountain.

At last, you will reach the bottom, pass through a gate, and be rewarded with a mostly downhill ride on FR 42's well maintained gravel and hard-packed dirt road. Once you reach Route 664, turn right and enjoy the feel of smooth pavement. Remember to keep some money on hand in case you need to stop at the convenience store (along Route 664 on your way back to Sherando).

This ride sequentially combines all types of mountain-bikeable terrain imaginable. It begins with smooth singletrack up White Rock Gap, then changes to a rocky trail along the slopes of Torry Ridge. Rocky, barren, forest roads pick up where the trails leave off, as you travel along the mountain tops of Big Levels. Once at the bottom, you will ride on FR 42, a well maintained gravel road. This leads you to pavement, and you're back where you started from.

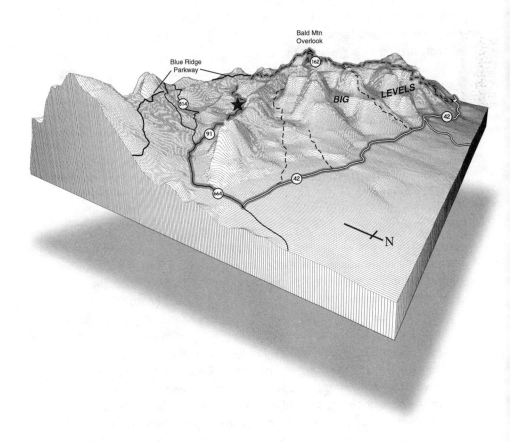

23. Henry Lanum Trail

Start: *AT parking area on 775*   **Terrain:** *Singletrack, jeep trails*
Length: *5.3 miles*   **Riding Time:** *1 – 1½ hours*
Rating: *Difficult*   **Other Uses:** *Hiking, Horseback*

Formerly known as the Pompey and Mount Pleasant Trail, this five-mile loop is well worth the trip to its somewhat remote location.

The Henry Lanum Jr. Trail has the reputation of being a "somewhere else to go" trail for outdoors people weary of the state's major trail systems and looking for a change of scenery. This well-marked course from start to finish is a loop not so heavily traveled, and consequently it offers people a bit more solitude.

However, for off-road cyclists, the Henry Lanum Jr. Trail is not just a place to go when Virginia's trails prove mundane. For daring and eager mountain bikers, this is a first-class loop of trails with more challenges and greater rewards than many trails more conveniently located and twice its size.

The trail is located nine miles east of Buena Vista, off U.S. Highway 60. Its remoteness is apparent after driving along the number of backroads north of U.S. 60 to the trailhead parking lot where this ride begins.

The loop is something of a spur to the Appalachian Trail, which crosses the dirt road at the trailhead parking lot. The lot itself was intended to be an access point for the Appalachian Trail. However, when Henry Lanum designed the Pompey and Mount Pleasant Loop, and developed it for public use, his vision was to create a beautiful diversion from the popular Appalachian Trail. He succeeded in doing so, personally maintaining this loop year-round. In July 1991, Lanum died while working on the Hidden Lake Trail in Idaho's Panhandle National Forest. In memory of Henry Lanum Jr., the Pompey and Mount Pleasant Trail was renamed and dedicated in his name. Because the Henry Lanum Jr. Trail is not actually a part of the Appalachian Trail, cyclists are welcome to ride here. Remember, bicycles are strictly prohibited on the Appalachian Trail.

This ride begins at the same trailhead parking lot that intersects with the Appalachian Trail. You could begin the loop by parking further down the road at the Henry Lanum Trail parking area, but there is more space in this lot, and the ride to the loop's start is

Moo.

recommended.

Follow the dirt road downhill momentarily until you see a grassy trail on the right that zips up into the woods. Follow this to another trail sign, where you will turn left and find yourself at the parking area and trailhead for the Henry Lanum Jr. Trail.

After riding this loop, it becomes apparent that unbearably steep climbs can be avoided if you travel in a counterclockwise direction. Follow the trail on the right side of the parking area (marked "Mount Pleasant") around the wooden trail gate and pedal into the woods on a flat, old logging road. This trail gradually ascends until it reaches the North Fork Creek and Cascades. At this point, the trail climbs rather abruptly toward Mount Pleasant. This climb lasts nearly one mile before you reach the top and pedal through a small meadow. You will ascend another one-half mile of steep, rocky terrain in order to reach the summit of Mount Pleasant (4,021 feet). This prominent peak offers an outstanding view of the Appalachian Mountains,

(continued on page 185)

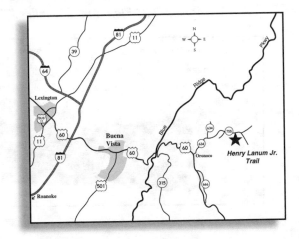

Henry Lanum Trail

☞   From I-81 near Lexington and Buena Vista – Take U.S. 60 east
through **Buena Vista** to **Route 634** at **Oronoco**. Turn **left** on **Route
634**. After approximately 1½ miles, bear **right** at the split on **Route 755**,
which changes to gravel. Follow this approximately 3 miles to **Hog Camp
Gap**, where the **Appalachian Trail** crosses. Park in the parking area on
the left side of the road. Route 755 becomes Route 48 here. •

MILES   DISTANCE

0.0   **START** from the **trailhead parking area** next to the Appala-
        chian Trail. Go east on **ROUTE 48**.

0.2   Just before Routes 48 and 635 split, there is a little grass
        trail that zips up the hill on the right side of the road. Marking
        this trail are three wooden posts with a blue square. Bear
        right off Route 48 on this **GRASSY TRAIL**, and follow it into
        the trees.

0.3   Come to a trail sign and a small wooden trail gate. Turn **left**,
        continuing to follow the **GRASSY TRAIL** to the start of the
        Henry Lanum Jr. Trail.

0.35 Cross Route 635 and enter a small parking area at the start
        of the **Henry Lanum Jr. Trail**.

        (Note: There are two trailheads at this parking area. Both
        trails lead into the woods. Take the trail on the **far right**
        marked **"Mt. Pleasant 2.6 miles."** This will take you around

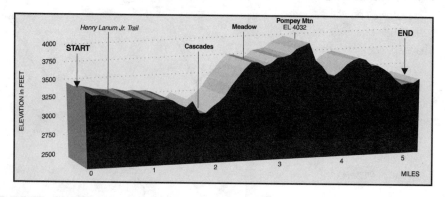

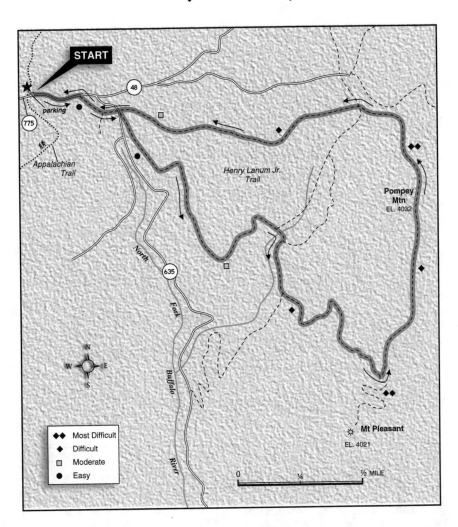

the loop in a counterclockwise direction. You can go either way. However, traveling in the counterclockwise direction helps make this loop much more manageable. The loop starts off as a flat wagon trail along the creek. Go around the wooden trail gate to begin.)

1.6   Arrive at the **cascades**. Cross the creek twice.

1.9   Start climbing toward Mount Pleasant.

2.7   The trail becomes level, crosses through a thick meadow, and reaches a wooden trail sign.

(Note: From this sign you may either continue this loop toward Pompey Mountain or detour one-half mile to the summit of Mount Pleasant. If you wish to make the one mile, round-trip effort to the top of Mount Pleasant, be aware that the trail is very steep and rocky. At 4,021 feet, though, the view is well worth the effort.)

3.4   Crest **Pompey Mountain** (4,032 feet). There's no real view from this mountaintop, but your climb is rewarded with a wild descent on a challenging, narrow trail.

3.8   This descent ends. Start climbing again. This climb is moderate compared with those preceding it.

4.3   Reach the top of this climb. The trail levels off, then begins a final descent to the beginning of the loop. This descent is very quick. Watch out for other trail users on your way down.

5.0   Return to the **Henry Lanum Jr. trailhead**. Ride back to the parking area the way you came.

5.3   Arrive at the parking area.

Ride Information

Trail Maintenance Hotline:

Pedlar Ranger District   (703) 261-6105
George Washington Ntl. Forest HQ   (703) 564-8300

Schedule:

Public land, accessible year-round

Maps:

USGS maps: Montebello, VA; Forks of Buffalo, VA
DeLorme: VA Atlas & Gazetteer – Page 54 B-2
GW National Forest topo map – Pedlar Ranger District

(continued from page 181)

and its 3,000-foot drop-off yields a mostly unimpaired view. Traveling to the top of this peak adds an extra mile to the loop.

The loop continues along the ridgetop upward to Pompey Mountain. No startling views or sweeping panoramas are visible from this mountaintop, but the thrilling descent on the other side compensates nicely. Ride this descent with extreme caution; the trail is extremely narrow and steep and is loaded with obstacles that can

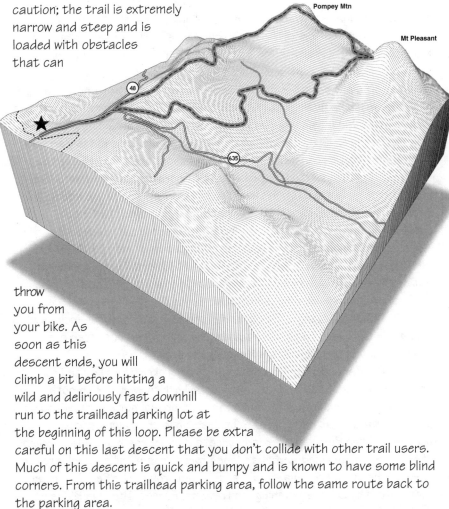

throw you from your bike. As soon as this descent ends, you will climb a bit before hitting a wild and deliriously fast downhill run to the trailhead parking lot at the beginning of this loop. Please be extra careful on this last descent that you don't collide with other trail users. Much of this descent is quick and bumpy and is known to have some blind corners. From this trailhead parking area, follow the same route back to the parking area.

If you're more interested in muscling this loop at a slower pace to capture its scenery, watch for patches of wildflowers, mountain laurel, blueberries, rhododendron, oak, hickory, and yellow birch. The trail winds through a garden of colorful flora and fauna.

24. Blue Ridge Dirt Ride

Start: *Buena Vista Overlook*	**Terrain:** *Forest roads, Blue Ridge Pkwy*
Length: *15.3 miles*	**Riding Time:** *2 hours*
Rating: *Moderate*	**Other Uses:** *Automobiles*

The Blue Ridge Parkway is 470 miles of quiet, beautifully designed roads rolling on top of the mountain peaks of the Appalachian Mountain Range. Construction began in 1935 near the Virginia-North Carolina border and continued north to Front Royal, Virginia. Today, the Parkway officially begins in Front Royal. The first segment opened in April of 1939, while the final section opened in 1987 with the completion of the Grandfather Mountain segment in North Carolina. Throughout its short history, nearly 600 million visitors have visited the Blue Ridge Parkway. That's almost 11 million visitors per year or more than 30,000 per day.

From Front Royal, Virginia, to the Cherokee Indian Reservation near Cherokee, North Carolina, the Blue Ridge Parkway is the scenic link between the Shenandoah National Park in Virginia and the Great Smokey Mountains of North Carolina and Tennessee. It follows the Appalachian's highest ridges, attaining altitudes of more than 6,000 feet while averaging between 3,000 and 4,000 feet. This magnificent national treasure was designed specifically for a leisurely and scenic route through this prominent mountain region.

This moderately difficult and extremely scenic loop is included in this guide to illustrate to mountain bikers an obvious but often over-looked asset of the Blue Ridge Parkway.

The Parkway, from Front Royal to Cherokee, is well suited for both bicycling tourists and day-cyclists alike. However, the smooth pavement and long, leisurely climbs may not appeal quite as much to the off-road rider. What many folks fail to realize is that along certain sections of the Parkway off-road cyclists can access hundreds of miles of both well maintained and abandoned forest roads, all of which are open to the public. Virginia's main access is through the Pedlar Ranger District of the George Washington National Forest. The Blue Ridge Parkway extends over more than 100 miles through this 147,000-acre section of public land and offers   countless points of access into the National Forest.

In addition to the   dramatic change of scenery,   from   skyline views along the

Views from the Blue Ridge Parkway.

Parkway to dense, old-growth forests surrounding the dirt roads, these forest routes afford cyclists the luxury to abandon their traffic woes and concentrate on nothing but the ride itself. There are seldom any vehicles to worry about, either in view or in earshot, and wildlife is often visible from every point of the ride. The lush green of the forest's thick undergrowth and splashy array of colorful wildflowers could hardly exist along the paved roads of the busy world beyond.

This loop starts from the Buena Vista Overlook on the Blue Ridge Parkway. Like most overlooks and access points, there's plenty of room to park the car. Pedal north up the Parkway a bit, then exit west on U.S. 60. This takes you right down to Forest Access Road 315.

Through the gate, this well maintained dirt road descends the mountain toward Pedlar River, for which this district of the forest is named. After a few ups and downs and more than seven miles of forested serenity, FR 315 comes to an end at FR 311. Unfortunately, most of these dirt roads don't have any signs or road names, so it's important to follow the maps closely, know your dis-

(continued on page 191)

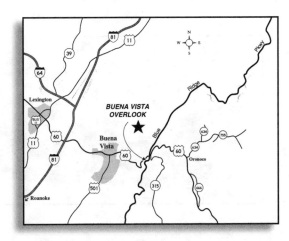

Blue Ridge Dirt Ride

☞   From I-81 near Lexington and Buena Vista – Take U.S. 60
(Buena Vista exit) east. Pass through Buena Vista on U.S. 60 east
and enter the George Washington National Forest. Climb up to the
Blue Ridge Parkway. Cross beneath the Parkway, then turn left on the
entrance ramp to access the Blue Ridge Parkway. Turn left on the Blue
Ridge Parkway heading south. Go approximately 0.5 miles to the Buena
Vista Overlook on the right.

MILES   DIRECTIONS

0.0   START at the Buena Vista Overlook on the Blue Ridge Park-
        way. Head north on the BLUE RIDGE PARKWAY to U.S. 60.

0.1   Cross over U.S. 60.

0.2   Exit the Blue Ridge Parkway to U.S. 60 East.

0.3   Turn left on U.S. 60 EAST through Humphreys Gap.

0.4   Turn right on FR 315. Go around the gate if it's closed. This
        dirt road winds up and down through the valley of Pedlar River.

3.4   Cross over Roberts Creek. An unnamed dirt road intersects
        with FR 315 at this point. Continue straight on FR 315. Reach
        the low point along FR 315 (1,390 feet).

4.5   Cross over Shady Mountain Creek. This, like Roberts Creek, is

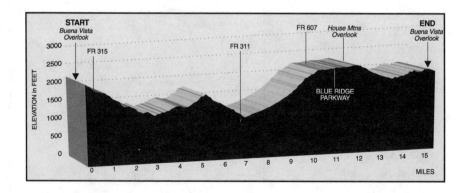

(continued from page 187)

tances, and carry a compass. There are so many miles of dirt roads back here that a wrong turn can get you completely spun around and headed in the wrong direction.

At FR 311, pass through a gate and begin climbing the slow but steady grade back toward the Parkway. At the top of this climb, pass through another gate and come to another intersection (FR 607). Turn right on this dirt road and notice the Blue Ridge Parkway on your left. FR 607 travels along the ridge for just over one mile, then ducks under the Parkway and heads down the west side of the mountain to Buena Vista. Unfortunately, FR 607 never directly accesses the Parkway. You

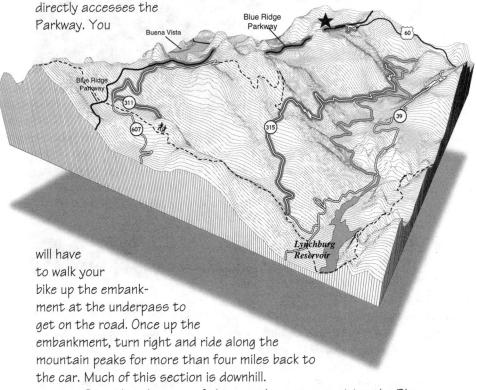

will have to walk your bike up the embankment at the underpass to get on the road. Once up the embankment, turn right and ride along the mountain peaks for more than four miles back to the car. Much of this section is downhill.

This ride is but one of the countless opportunities the Blue Ridge Parkway offers mountain bikers as it passes through this large segment of the George Washington National Forest. Please remember, of course, that while the Blue Ridge Parkway also travels through the Shenandoah National Park, just north of here, mountain bikes are not allowed within the Park's boundaries. Only National Forest land is open in Virginia to cyclists.

25. Potts Mountain

Start: *Hanging Rock parking*	**Terrain:** *Forest roads, hilly singletrack*
Length: *8.6 miles total*	**Riding Time:** *1 – 2 hours*
Rating: *Difficult*	**Other Uses:** *Hiking, Auto's (light)*

To get to Roanoke, the state's largest city west of Richmond, just follow the great star perched atop Mill Mountain. Roanoke, the self-titled "Star City of the South," lies on the banks of the Roanoke River at the southern end of the Shenandoah Valley and is flanked by both the Blue Ridge and Allegheny Mountains.

In earlier days Roanoke was just a small village known as Big Lick, named for the deer that sought out the area's salt deposits. With the arrival of the railroad industry, Big Lick grew into a town, and in 1882 two large railroads, the Shenandoah Valley Railroad and the Norfolk and Western, both built junctions along the Roanoke River. In 1884 Big Lick's population had grown past 5,000, and this western Virginia crossroads was chartered as the city of Roanoke.

The city thrived on coal, timber, and limestone from the nearby mountains until manufacturing railroad cars, textiles, and furniture, as well as building hardware, proved more profitable and enduring. Today Roanoke makes its claim as the capital of the Blue Ridge, enjoying all the wonders of a modern city. Unlike Virginia's other hubs, though, Roanoke is the only one fortunate enough to be nestled between the Blue Ridge and the Allegheny Mountains. What this means for people who enjoy both urban and rural lifestyles is that 4,000-foot peaks

Within these mountains lie many uncharted routes.

are only minutes from the Museum of Fine Arts, the Appalachian Trail passes by such natural wonders as Dragons Tooth and McAfee's Knob, just west of downtown Roanoke and, for mountain bikers in the region, hundreds of miles of trails and forest roads network through the endless acres of national forest land only a short drive away.

Potts Mountain is one such place near Roanoke that is regarded by off-road cyclists as a match made in heaven: its scenic forest roads and steep singletrack descents are only a short drive from Roanoke, and its forested terrain can entrance you for hours on end. Situated in the heart of the Jefferson National Forest, Potts Mountain rises to nearly 3,800 feet above sea level, with a ridge line nearly as sharp as nearby Dragons Tooth. The ride begins from the Hanging Rock parking area on FR 177 atop Potts Mountain's ridge.

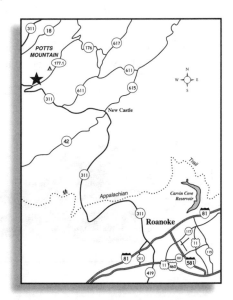

(continued on page 196)

Potts Mountain

☞   **From Roanoke** – Take **Exit 141** off I-81 to **Route 311 north** toward **New Castle** (18 miles). Continue on **Route 311** approximately 10 miles further to the top of **Potts Mountain**. Turn **right** off Route 311 on **FR 177** at the picnic area. Travel on **FR 177** for about 4.5 miles to the **Hanging Rock parking area**. Park here.

MILES   DIRECTIONS

0.0   **START** at the **parking area** for **Hanging Rock Overlook** on **FR 177**. Travel northeast along FR 177 toward Cove Trail.

1.1   Pass the old radio facility on the left. This resembles a large concrete bunker. Keep your eyes peeled for the trailhead sign on the right pointing to Cove Trail.

1.6   Turn **right** on **COVE TRAIL**. There should be a sign on the right with a hiker on it at this trailhead. Be ready for a steep descent into Potts Cove.

3.5   Reach the bottom of the descent and travel through Potts Cove.

3.6   Cross a small wooden bridge from the trail onto a gravel road. This road leads you up to FR 176.

4.2   Turn **left** on **FR 176**. This leads you uphill back to the top of Potts Mountain. Start climbing.

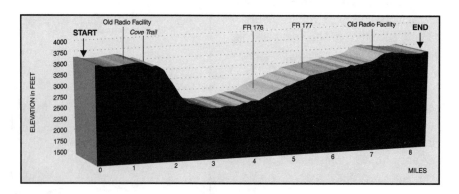

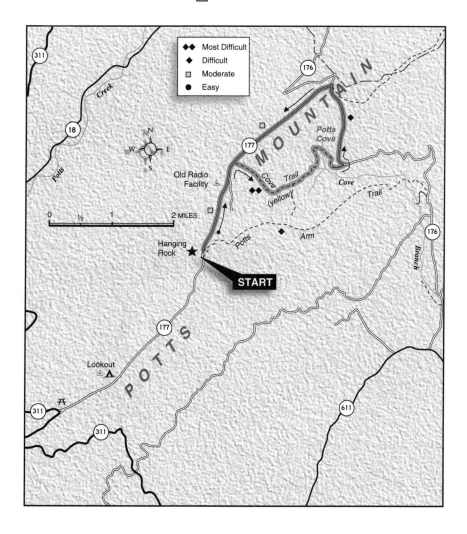

5.4 Reach the top. Turn **left** on **FR 177** at this intersection. There are some wonderful views from this road on either side of the mountain.

7.2 Pass the trailhead for Cove Trail.

7.6 Pass the concrete radio "bunker" on the right.

8.6 Reach the **Hanging Rock parking area**.

(continued from page 193)

There is a short trail from this parking lot to Hanging Rock Overlook. The overlook offers an incredible view of Hanging Rock Valley and is worth the extra time to make the hike.

From the parking area head north on FR 177. This gravel forest roads runs along the ridge of Potts Mountain past an old radio facility resembling a concrete bunker. One-half mile past this radio facility you will come upon a trail sign on the right. This is the sign for Cove Trail. Turn right on this trail and be ready for an incredibly quick and steep descent into Potts Cove. Be sure to follow the yellow blaze trail all the way. Cove Trail will lead you through Potts Cove for two miles, then cross over a small, wooden bridge and end up on a gravel road. This gravel road travels one-half mile to FR 176. Turn left on FR 176 and start climbing. This gravel forest road takes you back to the top of Potts Mountain.

Ride Information

Trail Maintenance Hotline:

New Castle Ranger District　　　(703) 864-5195
Jefferson National Forest HQ　　(703) 265-6054

Schedule:

Public land, accessible year-round

Maps:

USGS maps:　　Potts Creek, VA – WV
DeLorme:　　　　VA Atlas & Gazetteer – Page 52 D-1
Jefferson National Forest topo map – New Castle Dist.

Turn left on FR 177 at the top and follow this all the way back to Hanging Rock.

This ride is just a sample of the many different rides possible in this region. Ask the New Castle District Rangers about which trails are appropriate for riding. All of the forest roads are open to bicycling, but recently they have lost to private ownership the right-of-way to a number of trails.

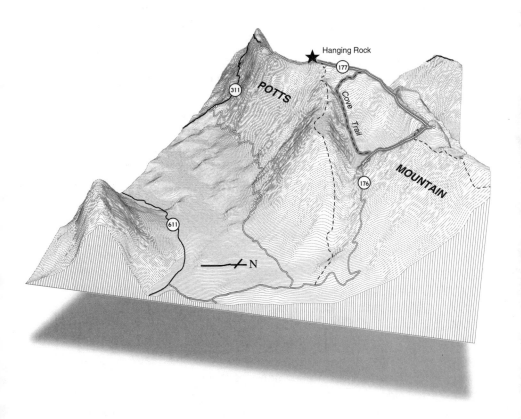

26. Brush Mountain

Start: *FR 188.2 off Rte 460*   **Terrain:** *Singletrack, gravel road*
Length: *8.3 miles*   **Riding Time:** *2 – 2½ hours*
Rating: *Difficult*   **Other Uses:** *Hiking, Horseback*

Picture in your mind the *perfect* mountain biking spot. Chances are, you'd be thinking of something that is, in fact, very similar to a place called Brush Mountain, located just north of the small Virginia college town of Blacksburg.

Brush Mountain has become, for nearly all off-road cyclists in this area, the quintessential mountain biking haven. Its proximity to town and campus—the mountain is cycling distance from Virginia Tech—makes Brush Mountain an ideal place for busy students to ride. They can easily spend an afternoon riding around the mountain's trails and still get back with plenty of time to hit the books at day's end. The mountain's convenient location, though, is not the only reason Brush Mountain is included in this guide. This mountain is also home to some of the finest off-road bicycling trails in the state of Virginia.

The Brush and Gap Mountain Multiple-Use Trails have not gone unrealized, as local clubs practice regular trail maintenance to preserve this mountain biking mecca. There are numerous waterbars strategically placed along the steep descents that protect the trails from excessive run-off and erosion. Trail corduroying, a method of repairing wet or muddy trails, is also evident throughout the mountain's trail system, further maintaining the trail's integrity from so much use. If you want to become more involved with trail maintenance, or just want some fun people to ride with, contact the friendly family at the East Coasters Bike Shop, down the road from Brush Mountain.

The closest access to the trails on Brush Mountain is from the Forest Service Road 188.2, just off Route 460. Take Route 460 west out of Blacksburg and start climbing (this is the east side of Brush Mountain). At the top of this climb there is a dirt road on the left side called FR 188.2. Follow this gravel-surfaced road up the steep hill and along the ridge of Brush Mountain.   This leads you all the way to the site of the old fire tower, a   circular drive at the end of the state-maintained service   road.

From this circular   drive, continue along the ridge of Brush   Mountain, on what is

If you're not part of the solution, then you're part of the problem.
To get involved with trail maintenance, just call these guys @
(703) 951-2369.

now an unmaintained jeep trail. Follow this trail along the ridge for one half-mile before reaching a three-way split. Notice, at this point, the red paint blazes on the trees. Turn right, following the red blazes into the woods, and begin your first wild descent toward Poverty Creek. Hold onto your brake pads as you descend through four very tight switchbacks, then straight down the west side of Brush Mountain.

At the bottom of the descent, this red-blazed trail comes to a "T," intersecting with the orange-blazed multiple-use trail. Turn right at this "T" and follow the smooth, flat singletrack trail alongside Poverty Creek. Be aware of hikers and equestrians also using this trail, and always yield the right-of-way. The orange paint blazes will lead you all the way back to FR 188.2 if you choose to complete this loop.

In just under one mile along the secluded Poverty Creek Multiple-Use Trail, you will reach a small opening. To follow this loop, you need to bear right into the woods, following the orange paint blazes. Bearing to the left will lead you to Gap Mountain, which has an entirely different network of great trails. To continue this loop, though, turn right and follow the orange blazes. These lead you toward Pandapas Pond. Please note that bicycles are not allowed within 300 feet of Pandapas Pond. There are a number of trails bordering the pond designed

(continued on page 203)

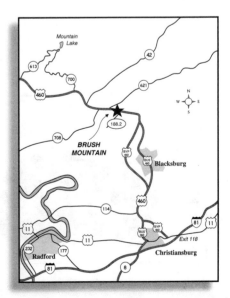

Brush Mountain

☞   From Blacksburg – Take **Main Street (Business Route 460)
west** toward Brush Mountain. Continue on **U.S. Highway 460 west** for
about 4 miles. At the top of the climb over **Brush Mountain**, turn **left** on
FR 188.2 (dirt road). Park wherever you can along FR 188.2 or go 2
miles along FR 188.2 to the old lookout tower and park.

MILES DIRECTIONS

0.0   **START** at **Forest Service Road 188.2**, just off U.S. Highway
      460. Head up the steep climb to the top of the ridge.

0.9   Pass the orange-blazed Brush Mountain Multiple-Use Trail on
      the right. Continue on **FR 188.2**.

1.9   Reach the remains of the **old lookout tower**. State mainte-
      nance ends at this point. Go **straight** through this circular
      drive, continuing into the woods on an old jeep trail.

2.5   The jeep trail splits. Turn **right** into the woods, following the
      red blazes. This leads to a fast, singletrack descent down to
      Poverty Creek.

      *(Note: Along the trail between the old lookout tower and this
      turn, you will ride through two semi-permanent mud holes
      before reaching this trail split. Turning left at this split drops
      you down the south side of Brush Mountain through private
      property. Straight takes you all the way to Boley Fields. Make
      sure to turn **right** (west) on the **red-blazed trail**.)*

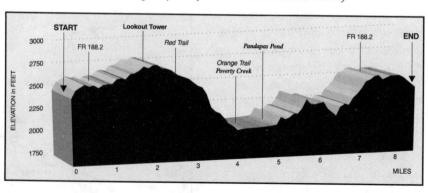

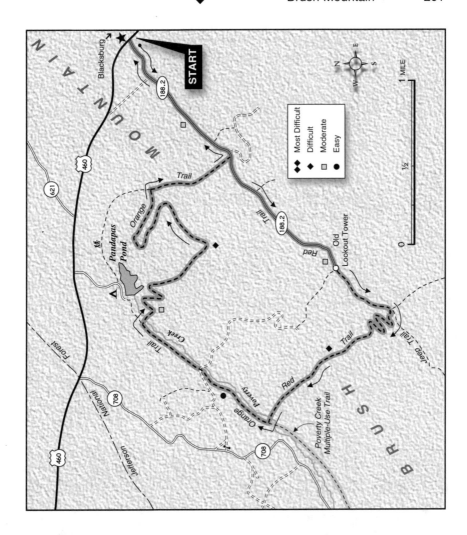

3.7 Reach the bottom of the descent.

3.75 Cross over **Poverty Creek**. This is a fairly dry creek crossing.

3.8 Turn **right** on the **POVERTY CREEK MULTIPLE-USE TRAIL (orange blaze)**. This well maintained, smooth singletrack trail parallels Poverty Creek.

4.6 Reach a small clearing. Bear **right** into the woods, following the **ORANGE BLAZE.** If you bear left into the open area, you will end up following trails that lead to Gap Mountain on the west side of Poverty Creek.

4.7   Arrive at a **4-way trail intersection**. Go **straight** through this trail intersection, following the **ORANGE DIAMOND BLAZES** tacked to the trees.

5.2   Turn **right** (southeast) across Poverty Creek on a narrow singletrack trail through a thick grove of rhododendron (orange blazes are slightly hidden). You've gone too far if you reach Pandapas Pond, 0.2 miles away.

5.85   This orange-blazed trail comes to a "T." Stay **left**, following the **orange blazes**.

5.85   The trail comes to another "T" (four orange blocks painted on a tree to the left). Take a **hard right** and start climbing.

6.5   Turn **right** on a wide jeep trail. This takes you uphill all the way back to FR 188.2.

7.4   Turn **left** on **FR 188.2**.

8.3   Reach **Route 406**.

Ride Information

Trail Maintenance Hotline:

Blacksburg Ranger District	(703) 552-4641
Jefferson National Forest HQ	(703) 265-6054
East Coasters Bike Shop	(703) 951-2369

Schedule:

Public land, accessible year-round

Maps:

USGS maps:	Blacksburg, VA; Newport, VA
DeLorme:	VA Atlas & Gazetteer – Page 41 B-6
Jefferson National Forest topo map – Blacksburg Dist.	

(continued from page 199)

exclusively for hikers. Be careful not to stray too far on the Poverty Creek Multiple-Use Trail and wind up at Pandapas Pond.

The orange trail turns right before the pond and crosses over Poverty Creek into a thick growth of rhododendron. From this point, all the way back to the ridge of Brush Mountain and FR 188.2, the trail weaves through heavy foliage, rolling up and down the mountain's western slope. This section is exciting enough to turn around at the jeep trail and grind it out a second

time.

Once at the jeep trail, turn right and climb your way back up to FR 188.2.

Because Brush Mountain is so close to town, the easiest way to get there may be by bicycle. There are few places to park aside from the circular drive at the old fire tower or along FR 188.2. Unfortunately, parking is severely limited on the mountain's peak and FR 188.2, while accessible to cars, is a gravel road with some large potholes. You may prefer to leave your car near the East Coasters Bike Shop, then ride the four miles uphill to the start. Another option is to park at the Pandapas Pond parking lot and walk your bike over to the main trail.

27. Mountain Lake

Start: *Mountain Lake Resort*   **Terrain:** *Hilly dirt roads, jeep trails*
Length: *21.4 miles*   **Riding Time:** *2½ – 3 hours*
Rating: *Moderate to Difficult*   **Other Uses:** *Automobiles, hiking*

Mountain Lake.

Mountain Lake, one of only two natural freshwater lakes in the state of Virginia (the other is Lake Drummond in the Great Dismal Swamp) and one of the highest lakes in the east, is home to the renowned Mountain Lake Resort. This romantic, sandstone resort has been a luxurious, year-round mountaintop getaway for nearly 200 years.

In 1986, the majesty of this grand old resort hotel was captured forever on film when it was used as the setting for the major motion picture *Dirty Dancing*, starring Patrick Swayze.

At nearly 4,000 feet above sea level, Mountain Lake's summers are cool and pleasant, making outdoor recreation ideal. Autumn brings with it an explosion of fall colors the likes of which few places compare. Even during the winters, when the mountains are filled with heavy snow, cross-country skiing and horse-drawn carriage rides keep guests busy and entertained.

The resort offers many guest activities on its 2,600-acre lot, and recently designated several miles of its wooded trails for mountain bikes. Tangent Outfitters of Dublin, Virginia, occupies a small shop at the resort and rents mountain bikes from the Lakeview Cottage. Guided mountain bike trips are also scheduled from the resort for those interested in exploring some of the area's more scenic spots. Maps detailing their trail systems are available from Mountain Lake Resort.

This fairly large loop, from Mountain Lake Resort to Butt Mountain, does not actually use any of the trails on the Mountain Lake Resort property. Instead, it leads cyclists on a more strenuous off-road journey deep into the Jefferson National Forest. This is a great ride for anyone interested in spending an afternoon mountain biking and who isn't afraid of a few hefty climbs along the way.

The terrain is hilly and the surface is, at times, rather rocky. Be prepared for a long ride. When you arrive at Butt Mountain Overlook, though, you are greeted with a panoramic view of the New River Valley and the vast stretches of land nearly 2,000 feet below, making all the effort worth your while. Perhaps the only lookout comparable in the entire region is the fabled McAfee's Knob, located north of Roanoke on the Appalachian Trail.

If you have any remaining energy past Butt Mountain, take time to depart from the main route and check out the cascading falls along Cascades Trail. Otherwise, continue along the jeep road down through Little Meadows, then climb uphill toward Route 613. This incredibly steep road heads back to Mountain Lake and was used as a brutal climb in the mountainous Stage Four of both the 1994 and 1995 editions of the Tour DuPont professional bicycle race. Many of the world's greatest cyclists struggled up Route 613 before making the harrowing, high-speed descent back down Route 700. American and World Champion Lance Armstrong was first to crest this Category-1 climb over Salt Pond Mountain at Mountain Lake Resort both years running, and in 1995 won the 141-mile stage from Lynchburg to Blacksburg with a solo break-away.

Chances are, after this ride, you may want to pedal directly into the 72-degree water of Mountain Lake. Afterwards, taste the superb cuisine in Mountain Lake's formal stone dining room. If you're visiting in autumn, help celebrate a traditional German Oktoberfest, held the last two Saturdays in September and each Friday and Saturday in October. So if you're interested in mountain biking on top of the world, Mountain Lake is, without question, the place to be.

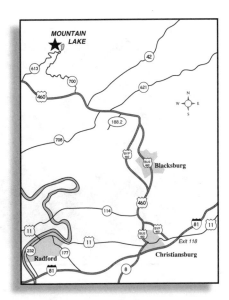

Mountain Lake

☞   From I-81 near Blacksburg — Take Exit-118 to U.S. 460 west to Blacksburg. Take U.S. 460 Bypass (left fork) around Blacksburg to Route 700. Turn right on Route 700, going seven miles uphill to Mountain Lake.

MILES   DIRECTIONS

0.0   **START** at **Mountain Lake Resort**. From the resort, follow the paved road (**ROUTE 613**) around the west side of the lake.

0.6   **ROUTE 613** changes to a **dirt road**.

1.5   Pass the **Mountain Lake Biological Station** on the right. This biological station is sponsored by the University of Virginia. Bear **left**, continuing on **ROUTE 613**.

3.2   Pass the parking area on the right for the **War Spur and Chestnut Trail**. These trails make a 4.5-mile loop through Jefferson National Forest's Mountain Lake Wilderness along Salt Pond Mountain Ridge. War Spur Overlook is fewer than two miles into this loop. Continue north on **ROUTE 613**.

4.1   Start climbing **Minnie Ball Hill**.

5.3   Reach the top of this climb (3,972 feet). Turn **left** on ROCKY MOUNTAIN ROAD at this intersection and follow the rocky jeep trail along the ridge of Big Mountain. There is a dirt

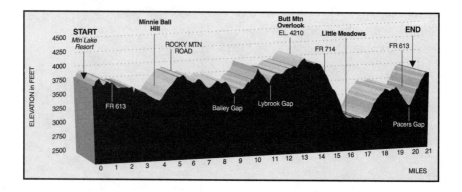

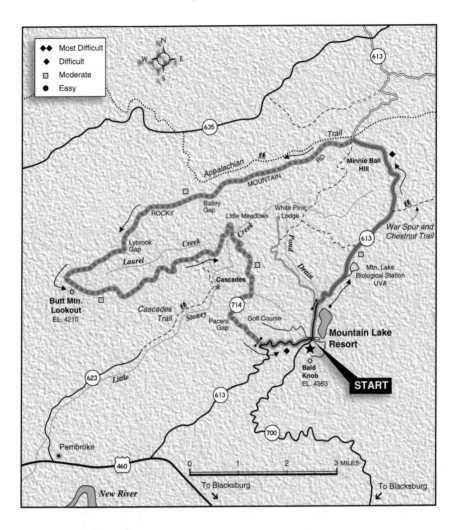

parking area at this intersection for the Appalachian Trail.

8.6 Go through Bailey Gap (3,637 feet).

10.9 Go through Lybrook Gap (3,794 feet).

13.0 Reach **Butt Mountain Overlook** (4,210 feet). Check out the incredible view of the New River Valley. Continue following the main dirt road (now **FR 714**). Get ready for a long, fast descent down to Little Meadows.

15.6 On the right is the trailhead for the **Cascades Trail**. Continue on **FR 714**.

16.0   Cross over **Laurel Creek**.

16.9   Pedal through **Little Meadows**.

17.1   Cross over **Little Stony Creek**. Get ready to start climbing again.

19.2   Go through Pacers Gap (3,635).

20.1   Turn **left** on **ROUTE 613** (paved). This is a very steep section of road that takes you back to the summit at Mountain Lake Resort. It is on this section of the climb that Lance Armstrong attacked in the 1995 Tour DuPont, breaking away for a solo victory in Blacksburg and claiming the race leader's yellow jersey.

21.4   Arrive at **Mountain Lake Resort**. What a ride!

Ride Information

Trail Maintenance Hotline:

Blacksburg Ranger District	(703) 552-4641
Jefferson National Forest HQ	(703) 265-6054
Mountain Lake Resort	1-800-346-3334

Schedule:

Open year-round

Maps:

USGS maps: Eggleston, VA; Interior, VA, WVA
Pearisburg, VA; Lindside, VA
DeLorme: VA Atlas & Gazetteer – Page 41 B-5
Jefferson National Forest topo map – Blacksburg Dist.

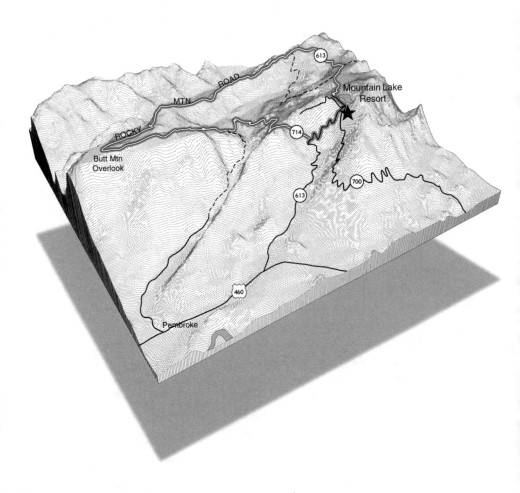

28. Mount Rogers Loop

Start: *Pull-off on FR 90*	**Terrain:** *Hilly fire roads, singletrack*
Length: *8.0 miles*	**Riding Time:** *2 hours*
Rating: *Difficult*	**Other Uses:** *Hiking, Horseback*

I was not the first to discover this ride. In fact, long before I arrived, countless hours had already been spent clearing the trails and marking this route. It's no accident, therefore, that this loop, used as the official race course for Virginia Highlands Mountain Bike Club's 1994 Mountain Bike Challenge, represents one of the finest mountain bike rides in Virginia.

Smooth singletrack, fast descents, spectacular overlooks and mountain meadows, winding dirt roads, and trails that grip the edges of steep ridges combine to form an extraordinary ride in the highlands of Southwest Virginia worthy enough to attract Virginia's best mountain bikers.

But this should come as no surprise since this loop is located within the boundaries of Mount Rogers National Recreation Area. Mountain biking is both welcome and encouraged inside this 115,000-acre mountain wilderness. Over 400 miles of open trails in the Mount Rogers National Recreation Area wind over high mountain peaks, across wind-beaten meadows, and along rushing highland streams. This is one of the east coast's wildest and most rugged regions and includes a number of Virginia's loftiest mountains. Is it any wonder mountain biking is taken so seriously down here?

Mount Rogers National Recreation Area is named for Virginia's highest peak, which stands at 5,729 feet. Whitetop Mountain, a close second, stands nearby at 5,520 feet and was so named because it is often covered with snow long after the snow has melted away in the valleys. The summit of Whitetop Mountain is also home to the highest vehicular road in the state. Route 89 takes cars from Route 600 on a spectacular uphill drive to the "balds," or open meadows, at the top of this lofty mountain.

Also near this loop is the Virginia Creeper Trail. This rail-trail travels 34 miles through the rugged landscape of Mount Rogers, from Abingdon to the Virginia-North Carolina border. If you're looking for a low-difficulty ride that passes over high-river gorges,

travels past waterfalls and rolling pastures, and crosses more than 100 bridges and trestles, then stay an extra few days and fit this unique trail into your schedule.

This particular loop, just off U.S. Highway 58, takes you up and over Iron Mountain. It begins on a well maintained dirt road and eventually becomes complete singletrack. Though most of the dirt roads you will encounter on this loop travel uphill, there will be occasions of extreme speed on white-knuckled descents. The loop's singletrack stretches up and down the mountain's ridges and, at times, grips the side of the mountain with barely a bike width of trail. Equestrians frequent these trails as well, so use caution when pedaling along these tight routes.

You will also notice along the route many different trails, all of which branch further into the National Recreation Area. Detailed area maps, useful for exploring the many trails in this vast, off-road playground, can be found at Highland Ski and Outdoor Center in Abingdon. Perhaps even set up a base camp at one of Mount Rogers

(continued on page 217)

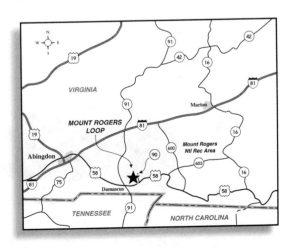

Mount Rogers Loop

☞   From Abingdon – Take U.S. 58 east to Damascus. From Damascus, continue on U.S. 58 for approximately 6 miles to FR 90. Turn left on FR 90 (dirt road) and park along the side of the road at the small pull-off.

MILES   DIRECTIONS

0.0   START from the pull-off on the right-hand side of FR 90, off U.S. Highway 58. Begin climbing this hard-packed, dirt road.

0.5   To the right is a great view of Whitetop Mountain. Just up the road is a gated fire road.

0.6   Turn left and pedal around the gate on a grassy FOREST ROAD. This forest road winds slowly uphill.

0.9   Turn right on a slightly hidden SINGLETRACK TRAIL up a short, steep hill.

       (Note: To find this trailhead, follow the grassy fire road uphill for 0.3 miles from FR 90. As you round the third curve (this will be curving left), there is a large hickory tree and a small creek on the right side of the road at the apex of the turn. The hickory tree marks the trailhead for this path. The climb up this trail is very steep, but is less than one tenth of a mile.)

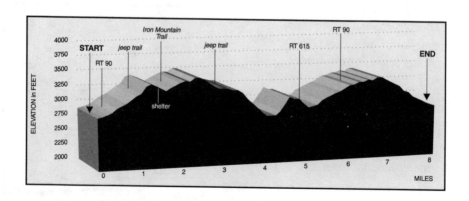

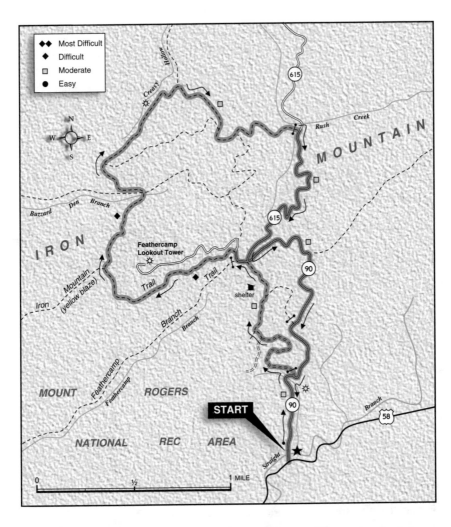

1.0 Reach the top of the steep, singletrack climb and turn **right** on a **WIDE, SINGLETRACK TRAIL.**

1.4 Small clearing on the right. Continue **straight** (bear left) on the **WIDE, SINGLETRACK TRAIL.**

1.5 Arrive at an **intersection of trails.** There is a shelter and picnic area on the left. To the right is a trail with man-made steps that heads up the mountain. Continue **straight** on the trail you're already on and descend toward FR 90.

1.6 Arrive at an intersection between FR 90 and FR 615. FR 90 crosses from right to left. FR 615 bears a soft right and heads downhill. Turn **left** on **FR 90** and follow this uphill to Iron Mountain Trail (yellow blaze). Note Feathercamp Branch Trail past the gate on the far left. Feathercamp Branch Trail travels downhill along grassy terrain for nearly two miles to U.S. 58.

1.7   Turn **left** on **IRON MOUNTAIN TRAIL (yellow blaze)**. This trail climbs gently up Feathercamp Ridge, skirting the ridgeline. The surface of this trail is smooth and well maintained.

2.4   Reach the top of the climb and begin a quick descent.

2.7   Arrive at a "T." Turn **right**, continuing to loop clockwise around this course. Turning left takes you west along Iron Mountain Trail, traveling along the crest of Feathercamp Ridge. Note the large oak tree marked with a yellow blaze.

3.2   Cross Buzzard Den Branch. This section of trail at the bottom of the descent is often very muddy. This trail is also used by equestrians, and you will notice the deep imprints of horse shoes in the wet soil.

Ride Information

Trail Maintenance Hotline:

Mount Rogers National Rec. Area   (703) 783-5196

Jefferson National Forest HQ   (703) 265-6054

Schedule:

Public land, accessible year-round

Maps:

USGS maps: Konnarock, VA

DeLorme: VA Atlas & Gazetteer – Page 22 C-3

Mount Rogers National Recreation Area topo map

Trees shaped by the high-mountain winds.

Reach the low point along this loop. **Bear right** up a very short trail. This takes you to a larger trail intersection.

3.35 At this trail intersection, turn **hard-left** on the **FOREST ROAD**.

3.8   Overview on the left.

4.6   Pedal across a small meadow.

5.0   Cross through a steel gate and turn **right** on **FR 615**. Start climbing.

6.1   Turn **hard-left** on **FR 90**. This takes you back to the start of the ride. Not done climbing yet!

6.5   Reach the summit of this climb on FR 90. Get ready for a fast descent!

6.8   Spectacular view of **Whitetop Mountain** to the south.

8.0   Reach the start of the ride at the bottom of FR 90.

DCR

Riding horseback in Virginia's high country. (Remember, horses spook easily. Always yield to equestrians, and consider dismounting and walking your bike to pass.)

(continued from page 211)

National Recreation Area's many campsites and spend the weekend riding as many new trails as possible. Because of this area's inspiring scenery and its hundreds of miles of rideable trails, very few places in the state can compare to this mountain biking wonderland.

29. New River Trail State Park

Start: *Pulaski Station*
Length: *51.5 miles total*
Rating: *Easy*

Terrain: *Flat, hard-packed gravel surface*
Riding Time: *Varies with distance*
Other Uses: *Hiking, Horseback*

Virginia has long been a leader in park development. On June 15, 1936, for example, it became the first state to open an entire park system on the same day. When Norfolk Southern Corporation donated a 57-mile section of railroad right-of-way between Pulaski and Galax to the Virginia Department of Conservation and Recreation in December 1986, the state again took the lead in park development and created its first linear greenway and certainly one of its most unique parks.

Some of the tunnels reach up to 200 feet long.

Southwestern Virginia's New River Trail follows the 57-mile abandoned railroad bed from Pulaski to Galax with a branch trail that leads to the town of Fries. For nearly 40 miles, this rail-trail parallels the banks of the New River, the great grandfather of rivers. The New River is much older than its name implies: flowing south to north, as very few rivers in North America do, the New River has the distinction of being the world's second oldest river.

Along the trail, cyclists will cross more than 30 bridges and trestles and cycle through tunnels nearly 200 feet long. The longest bridge in the park, located at Fries Junction, is over 1,000 feet long and offers dramatic views of this ancient river, which courses more than 40 feet below. Scenery unique to Southwest Virginia is visible along the way. The area's rich history of an era long past, with the departure of the railroad, lives on wholeheartedly in the towns and communities that line the trail.

The railroad was built in the late 1800s by the Norfolk and Western Railway Company to transport what was believed to be a

DCR

wealth of quality minerals in Wythe County, a cache larger than any other in the United States. Work on the railway began in Pulaski on December 10, 1883, and in 1890 much of the rail line reached well into Carroll County near Galax.

Blast furnaces were erected, massive supplies of minerals mined, thousands of tons of iron ore produced, and "boom towns" developed in numbers along the railroad as the industry prospered. Most of these towns still exist today.

As the hills emptied and the mines played out their last supplies, the railway became less and less profitable for the Norfolk Southern Corporation. Finally, in 1986, the decision came to abandon this stretch of railroad and donate the right-of-way to the state for a new purpose.

With the help of volunteer groups throughout Virginia, the park was able to open four miles of trail in May of 1987. Approximately 40 miles of this rails-to-trails park

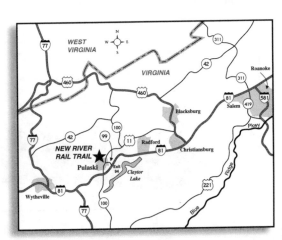

(continued on page 225)

New River Trail State Park

☞   **From Roanoke** – Take I-81 south to **Exit-94** and head **north** on **Route 99** approximately 2 miles into **Pulaski**. Immediately before the first red light there is a sign for the **Northern Terminus**. Parking is available.

Other Trail Entrances:

Draper Station (mile 6.2) – From I-81, take Route 658 east through Draper. Parking is available across from Bryson's Store, less than one mile from I-81.

Shot Tower Historical State Park (New River Trail Headquarters, mile 25.2) – From I-77, take Exit 24, go east on Route 69 to U.S. 52 and follow signs to Shot Tower.

Buck Dam (mile 34.7) – Take Route 602 to Byllesby, then go north on Route 737 to the dam.

Byllesby Dam (mile 37.3) – Go east on Route 602 off Route 94. Park at the dam.

Gambetta and Chestnut Yard (mile 45.2) – Take Route 721 north past Cliffview.

Cliffview Station (mile 49.5) – Take U.S. 58 to Galax, then go north on Route 887 to Cliffview Road (Route 721). Parking is on the left, across from Cliffview Mansion and Cliffview Trading Post.

Galax Station (mile 51.5) – Parking is available where U.S. 58 crosses Chestnut Creek.

(Note: At the time this book went to print, the New River Trail had not completely opened. An eight-mile section between Route 100 and I-77 is still under development and is closed to the public. You can restart your trip at Shot Tower and travel south all the way to Galax or Fries.)

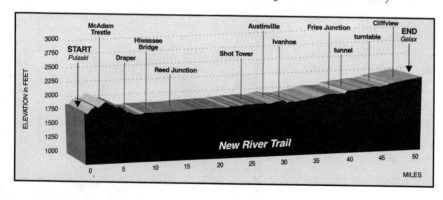

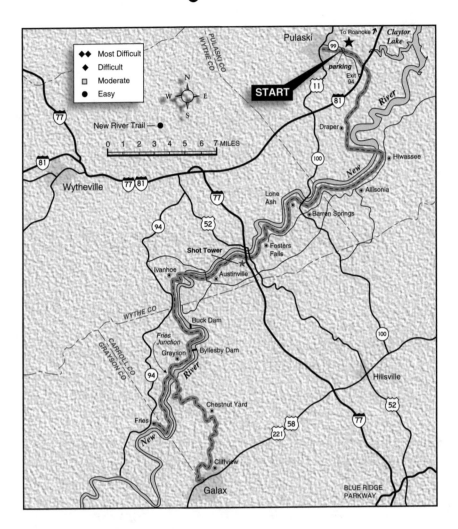

MILES DIRECTIONS

0.0 Restored Pulaski Station.

2.0 **START** at the **Dora Junction** just off Route 99 into Pulaski.

2.5 Peak Creek Trestle.

3.6 I-81 Overpass.

3.8 McAdam Trestle.

6.2   **Draper Station**. Parking, food, ranger station, restrooms available.

8.0   Delton Trestle.

8.1   Site of Clarks Ferry (stopped operating in 1939).

9.0   Delton. Convenience store and campgrounds available.

10.2 Cross **Hiwassee River Bridge** (951 feet long) to the east side of the New River.

12.6 **Allisonia Station**. Convenience store located along the trail.

13.2 Big Reed Trestle over Big Reed Island Creek.

14.2 Reed Junction.

17.4 Barren Springs Furnace. Built in 1883, it produced more than five tons of pig iron each day.

17.8 Barren Springs Station.

Ride Information

Trail Maintenance Hotline:

New River Trail State Park HQ   (703) 699-6778

Schedule:

Open daylight to dark all year-round

Maps:

USGS maps: Radford South, VA; Dublin, VA
     Hiwassee, VA; Fosters Falls, VA; Max Meadows, VA
     Sylvatus, VA; Austinville, VA; Galax, VA
DeLorme: VA Atlas & Gazetteer – Page 40 D-4, 24

Also Available:

Guide to the New River Trail State Park
$4.00 (postpaid) from Custom CADmaps
Rt. 1 Box 117-A1 Draper, VA 24324

View from the New River Valley.

19.0   Lone Ash.

20.3   Bertha.

22.7   Pass over the stone arch. This was built over a local farmer's spring box so that he could continue refrigerating his food and milk.

24.3   Fosters Falls.

25.2   **Shot Tower.** New River Trail Sate Park Headquarters. Parking, information, and restrooms. Shot Tower was built in the early 1900s to make shot for guns used by local hunters and soldiers in the Civil War. Molten metal was dropped 150 feet from the top of the tower into a kettle of cooling water below. It was thought that 150 feet was the distance necessary to shape falling molten lead into shot.

28.9   Austinville. Named after Moses Austin, father of Stephen Austin. Stephen Austin is known as the "Father of Texas," thus imparting his name to the lone-star state's capital.

31.6   Ivanhoe Depot. Convenience store near trail. (Ivanhoe Bridge is 670 feet long.)

32.6   Jubilee Park.

34.7   **Buck Dam**.

37.3   **Byllesby Dam**.

38.6   Grayson sulfur springs. Once a health resort touting its natural spa, the waters here were thought to cure ailments and skin diseases. The site of the old-time spa is now under water.

39.4   Grayson. Nearby restrooms and picnic area available.

39.8   **Fries Junction**. The New River Trail splits here and heads to either Fries or Galax (longest bridge along this trail at 1,089 feet long).

43.3   State Route 721 (Fries Branch).

45.3   Fries. Parking, information, and picnic area available (Fries Branch).

40.1   Site of 1928 train wreck that killed three people and injured nine.

40.3   Pass through a tunnel 229 feet long.

42.3   Gambetta.

45.1   Turntable site. The railroad line once ended here before being extended all the way to Galax. The turntable was used to turn trains around so they could head north again toward Pulaski.

45.2   **Chestnut Yard**.

46.3   Chestnut Creek Falls.

49.5   **Cliffview Station**. Parking, restrooms, information, horse and bicycle rental, ranger station, and food available.

51.5   **Galax Station**. Located off the main trail. Parking available.

(continued from page 219)

has since been opened to the public, and the rest is on its way. At the time this guide was published, the only remaining section to be finished was between mile marker 17 at Route 100 and mile marker 25 near Shot Tower.

　　　With so many places along the route to park your car and access the trail, there's no need to attempt riding the entire trail in one day. Pick different sections with each visit and explore the beauty and history of one of Virginia's finest rail-trails and most unique state parks.

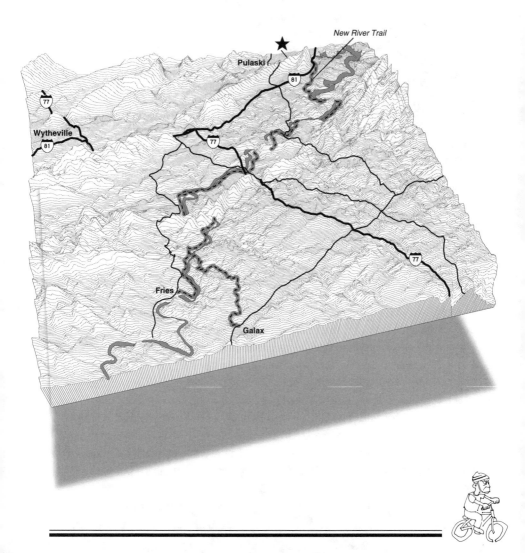

30. Virginia Creeper Trail

Start: *Abingdon Station*	**Terrain:** *Flat, hard-packed, gravel surface*
Length: *33.4 miles total*	**Riding Time:** *Varies with distance*
Rating: *Easy*	**Other Uses:** *Hiking, Horseback*

For hundreds of years, this ancient route was used by Native Americans as a footpath through the high mountains of the Appalachians. In 1900 the first locomotive chugged along this route from Abingdon Station to Damascus. By 1914, the railroad extended over even more of this ancient foot trail, all the way to Elkland, North Carolina. For over 75 years Locomotive #433 crept its way across rivers and gorges and up the steep grades of Virginia's highlands to collect timber, iron ore, passengers, and supplies. By 1977, due to economic hardships incurred as far back as the Great Depression, the Virginia Creeper (Locomotive #433) could not survive. Salvage rights for the rail line were subsequently sold to willing bidders. One year later, after the U.S. Forest Service purchased the right-of-way from Damascus to the Virginia-North Carolina border, work began to restore this scenic pathway. A few years later, Damascus and Abingdon bought the rest of the old railway. Today, 34 miles of this ancient Native American footpath has come full-circle and is, once again, a public trail open for all to enjoy.

The Virginia Creeper Trail begins in Abingdon, in Southwest Virginia,

Jim Carpenter

Whitetop Mountain dominates the landscape.

and stretches 34 miles through striking scenery over some of the
state's most rugged land before ending at the Virginia-North Carolina
border. The trail's waterfalls, deep river gorges, wildlife, rolling pastures,
and more than 100 bridges and trestles compose one of America's
premier rail-trails.

Mountain biking happens to be one of the most popular activities on the trail. The surface is smooth and cinder covered, with a
terrain that never exceeds a grade of more than six percent. The trail
only becomes steep when it crosses Whitetop Mountain, Virginia's
second highest peak, and heads to its highest point of 3,600 feet at
the Whitetop Station. One way to avoid this demanding aerobic workout
is to take the Blue Blaze Shuttle Service from Abingdon up to the
Whitetop parking area. The shuttle will transport both you and your bike,
and allows cyclists a carefree and easy downhill ride from Whitetop
Station all the way back to Abingdon. More information is available at
Highland Ski and Outdoor Center in Abingdon, which also rents bikes.

One point to
remember when cycling
the Virginia Creeper is
that the right-of-way
passes through some
areas of private property.
Local landowners ask
that you shut gates
behind you and respect
their property as you ride
along the trail.

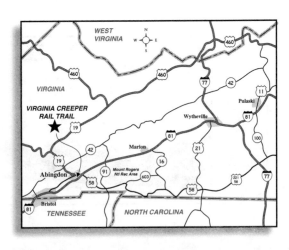

Virginia Creeper Trail

☞   **From Roanoke** – Take I-81 south to **Exit-8** in **Abingdon**. Go **north** on **Alternate 58** to **Main Street** and turn **right**. Pass Martha Washington Inn and the historic Barter Theater before turning **right** on **Pecan Street**. The trail begins at the **old locomotive** on display at the trailhead.

Other Trail Entrances:

Damascus (mile 15.5) – Take **U.S. 58** east from **Abingdon** to **Damascus**. Once in Damascus, follow **U.S. 58** through the town to the **red caboose** on the right. Parking available at this trailhead.

Green Cove Station (29.3) – From the intersection of U.S. 58 and Route 91 outside Damascus, take **U.S. 58 east**. Stay **right** on **U.S. 58** at the intersection with Route 603 and go 4.2 miles to Green Cove Road (FR 600). Turn **right** on **Green Cove Road** and follow this to **Green Cove Station**. Parking available.

Whitetop Station (mile 32.3) – Follow the above directions on U.S. 58 to Route 603. Stay **right** on **U.S. 58** and go 6.2 miles to Fire House Road (FR 755). Turn **right** on **Fire House Road** and go approximately 2 miles to the **Whitetop** parking area.

MILES   DISTANCE

0.0   **START** at the **Abingdon Trailhead**. Limited **parking**.

1.0   Cross under **I-81**.

1.3   Pass the Glenrochie Country Club.

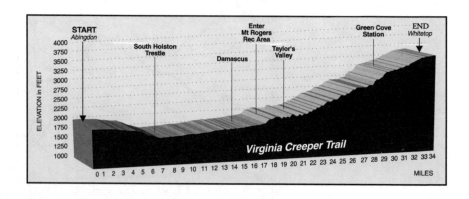

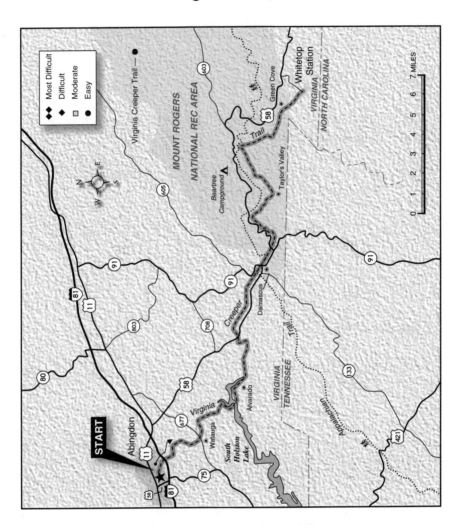

2.9 Cross **Route 677** in **Watauga**. Limited **parking**.

3.7 Walk or ride across the **Dry Branch Trestle**.

7.2 Walk or ride across the **South Holston Trestle**—very scenic. It spans the northern point of South Holston Lake where the south and middle forks of the Holston River converge. This is the lowest point on the Virginia Creeper Trail (1900 feet).

8.5 Arrive in the town of **Alvarado**. Limited **parking**.

15.5 Arrive in the town of **Damascus**. The big, red caboose is a U.S.

Forest Service **information station**. Limited **parking**. **Restrooms** in the town park.

16.9   Cross **Route 91**. Be careful, traffic is fast on this highway.

17.5   Ride across the **Iron Bridge**. Enter **Mount Rogers National Recreation Area**.

19.5   Reach the **Straight Branch parking lot** on the right. The Appalachian Trail goes off to the left.

21.0   Arrive in **Taylor's Valley**. There is a **vending** area on the left. Go through the gate. The river is on your right. Limited **parking**.

21.4   Walk or ride across this **trestle**.

24.0   Pass through **Konnarock Junction**. Limited **parking**.

25.0   Walk or ride across **High Trestle**. Crossing this 550-foot-long trestle can be a bit unnerving as it is more than 100 feet above the ground!

Ride Information

Trail Maintenance Hotline:

Mount Rogers Ntl. Rec. Area	(703) 783-5196
Abingdon Convention & Visitors Bureau	1-800-435-3440
Rails-to-Trails Conservancy	(202) 797-5400

Schedule:

Open daylight to dark all year-round

Maps:

USGS maps: Abingdon, VA; Damascus, VA; Konnarock, VA; Whitetop Mountain, VA Grayson, TN, VA; Park, NC, VA

DeLorme: VA Atlas & Gazetteer – Page 22 C-1

Virginia Creeper Trail trail map

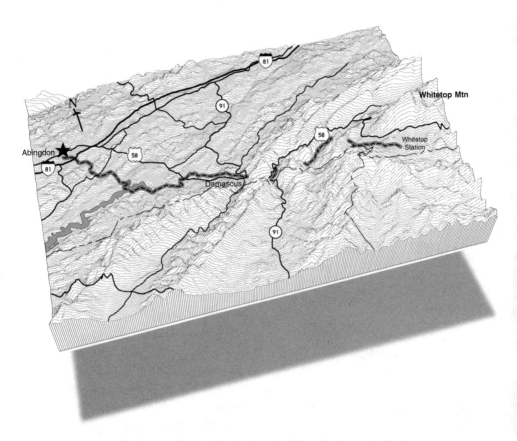

Whitetop Mtn

N

Abingdon

Damascus

Whitetop Station

25.4   The **Appalachian Trail** joins the Virginia Creeper Trail.

25.8   The Appalachian Trail goes left, deep into the Mount Rogers National Recreation Area.

27.2   Walk or ride across a small **trestle**.

29.3   Arrive at the old **Green Cove Station**. There is a seasonal U.S. Forest Service **information station** located here. There is also a **portable toilet** and limited **parking** available.

32.3   Arrive at **Whitetop Station**. This is the highest point on the trail (3,576 feet). Limited **parking**.

33.4   **Virginia-North Carolina border**. This is the end of the Virginia Creeper Trail.

Honorable Mentions

It would be tough to map every one of Virginia's off-road bicycle rides into a single guidebook. There are far too many. Therefore, it is necessary to chart only the best mountain bike rides the state has to offer, delegating other popular places for mountain biking to *Honorable Mention* status. And still, somehow, only a mere fraction of Virginia's rides are included. Compiled below is an index of great rides that did not make the A-list this time around, but deserve recognition. Check them out and let me know what you think. You may decide one or more of these rides deserves higher status in future editions, or, perhaps, you may have a ride of your own that merits some mentioning.

(A) Edinburg Gap. The George Washington National Forest Service has, in the last few years, recognized operating off-road vehicles as a valid use of forest land, and, consequently, has identified and constructed a number of All-Terrain Vehicle trails for four-wheel drive vehicles, motorcycles, and motorbikes. These **ATV trails** also provide excellent mountain biking, as cyclists will find miles of narrow, twisting routes coupled with wide, inviting paths, all of which are clearly labeled and easy to follow. In the Lee Ranger District at Edinburg Gap, there are two such trail systems: Peters Mill Run and Tasker Gap. Both systems can be accessed from Route 675 southeast of Edinburg. Signs will direct you from Route 675, onto the ATV Trails. Maps are available from the U.S. Forest Service in Edinburg @ **(703) 984-4101**. For a detailed map, see the ***DeLorme Atlas & Gazetteer*, page 73 B-7**.

(B) Second Mountain ATV Trails. Located approximately 10 miles west of Harrisonburg, off U.S. 33, near Rawley Springs. You could spend an entire day pounding yourself on these rocky, mountainous ATV trails atop Second Mountain in the George Washington National Forest. The trails, though steep and rugged, are clearly marked from the ATV parking area at the top of Second Mountain from FR 72. Follow the signs from the parking area onto the dozens of miles of trails. Be prepared for hours of off-road challenges. For a detailed map, see the *DeLorme Atlas & Gazetteer*, page 72 D-4.

C Great North Mountain Trail to Elliot Knob. Head
due west for 12 miles on Route 254 from Staunton to Buffalo Gap. There is trailhead parking at Dry Branch Gap on State Route 688. *This is not a trail for beginners.* The trail starts on an old logging road and follows the Great North Mountain ridgeline to Elliot Knob (4,463 feet), one of the highest points in the George Washington National Forest. Plan to scramble over narrow paths and rugged terrain, attain high speeds on hair-raising descents, and climb stiff ascents to panoramic views. Schedule at least four hours for this eight-mile round trip. For a detailed map, see the *DeLorme Atlas & Gazetteer*, page 66 C-1.

D Sugarloaf Mountain Ride. This is a wonderful backroads
ride through the foothills of the Blue Ridge Mountains, located approximately 20 miles south of Charlottesville off U.S. 29. From Rockfish Road (Route 617), turn right on Route 623, then left on Route 640 (Wheeler Cove Road). Route 640, a scenic dirt road, winds through Thoroughfare Gap. Turn right on Dutch Creek Road (Route 641) toward Sugarloaf Mountain. A jeep road leads you from Route 641 to the top of Sugarloaf Mountain. This three-mile ascent, however, is incredibly steep, but a breathtaking view awaits at the top. For a detailed map, see the *DeLorme Atlas & Gazetteer*, page 55 B-5.

E Appomattox-Buckingham State Forest. Located
30 miles east of Lynchburg off State Route 24. Part of Virginia's Piedmont Forest System, there are over 19,700 acres of rolling terrain. Miles of unpaved forest roads, trails, and dead-end paths wind through this pine and hardwood forest, most of which are ideal for off-road bikes. Holliday Lake State Park is situated within the forest with information, bathhouse, restrooms, camping, and showers. For a detailed map, see the *DeLorme Atlas & Gazetteer*, page 45 A-6. (804) 983-2175.

(F) **Prince Edward-Gallion State Forest.** Located off U.S. 460, 16 miles east of Farmville, 48 miles west of Petersburg. Also part of Virginia's Piedmont Forest System, there are nearly 7,000 acres of forested terrain with miles of unpaved forest roads and a three-mile bicycle trail near Twin Lakes State Park. Bike rentals are available. For a detailed map, see the *DeLorme Atlas & Gazetteer*, page 46 C-2. (804)492-4121.

(G) **Pocahontas State Forest.** Just minutes from Richmond, these 7,600 acres of Piedmont forest surround Pocahontas State Park (**see Ride #9**). Like Virginia's other state forests, Pocahontas has many miles of unpaved forest roads and trails, most of which are ideal for mountain biking. For a detailed map, see the *DeLorme Atlas & Gazetteer*, page 48 B-1. (804) 796-4250.

(H) **South Pedlar ATV Trails.** Situated on the Pedlar Ranger District of the George Washington National Forest, this is a looping network of nearly 25 miles of ATV-designed trails. The many narrow, twisting trails that make up this ATV trail system are popular among mountain bikers from Lynchburg, Buena Vista, and Lexington. Located one-half mile west of the Blue Ridge Parkway off Route 130. For a detailed map, see the *DeLorme Atlas & Gazetteer*, page 54 D-1 and U.S. Forest Service's trail map. (703) 261-6105.

(I) **North Mountain Trail near Roanoke.** A trail that Roanoke's hard-core mountain bikers often frequent when they're feeling aggressive. Fewer than 10 miles west of Roanoke on Route 311, you can access this trail in the New Castle Ranger District of the Jefferson National Forest from the road. Narrow, rugged singletrack follows the North Mountain ridge nearly 12 miles north. There are some smaller trails that fall down the west side of North Mountain to FR 224, a forest road that may give you the relief you need to get back to the start of this ride. For a detailed map, see the *DeLorme Atlas & Gazetteer*, page 42 A-2 or the New Castle Ranger District topography map @ (703) 864-5195.

J **Mountain Lake Mountain Bike Trails.** In 1994, Mountain Lake Resort (**see Ride #27**), north of Blacksburg, Virginia, designated nearly 10 miles of its trails for use by mountain bikes. Guests can rent mountain bikes from the Lakeview Cottage on a half-day and full-day rental basis and take guided trips to some of the Mountain Lake region's most scenic areas. All cyclists interested in riding the trails must get bicycle trail passes from the bike shop in Lakeview Cottage. A trail map is also available. For a detailed map, see the *DeLorme Atlas & Gazetteer*, page 41 B-5. (703) 626-7121.

K **Grayson Highlands State Park.** This unique state park in the rugged mountains of Southwestern Virginia is situated within Mount Rogers National Recreation Area (**see Ride #28**). In 1994, Grayson Highlands State Park opened its first Mountain Bike Trail System in the Wilson Creek drainage area. Much of the ride will run at nearly 4,000 feet and include stunning scenery, rugged trails, and two stream crossings. There are four access points to this trail from the park entrance road (Route 362). For a detailed map and more information on the trail, contact Grayson Highlands State Park @ **(703) 579-7092** or see the *DeLorme Atlas & Gazetteer*, page 23 D-5.

Northern Virginia Rides. To find out more about mountain biking in Northern Virginia, pick up *The Washington-Baltimore Mountain Bike Book.* Of the 25 off-road rides featured in *The Washington-Baltimore Mountain Bike Book*, 10 are in Northern Virginia. Rides ranging from leisurely lakeside trails minutes from the Beltway to off-road adventures beneath this urban sprawl's network of power lines are included in this *Atlas of the Washington-Baltimore Area's Greatest Off-Road Bicycle Rides.*

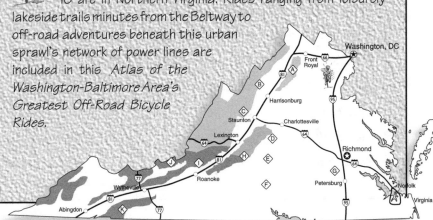

Ski Resorts

...for mountain biking?

Ski resorts offer a great alternative to local trail riding. During the spring, summer, and fall, many resorts will open their trails for mountain biking and, just like during ski season, sell lift tickets to take you and your bike to the top of the mountain. Lodging is also available for the weekend mountain bike junkies, and rates are often discounted from the normal ski-season prices. Many resorts even rent bikes and lead guided mountain bike tours. Call ahead to find out just what each resort offers in the way of mountain bike riding, and pick the one that best suits your fancy.

Below is a list of all the ski resorts in and around Virginia that say *yes!* to mountain biking when the weather turns too warm for skiing.

Massanutten	Harrisonburg, VA	(703) 289-9441
Wintergreen	Waynesboro, VA	(804) 325-2200
The Homestead	Hot Springs, VA	(703) 839-5500
Bryce	Basye, VA	(703) 856-2121
Wisp	McHenry, MD	(301) 387-4911
Timberline	Davis, WV	1-800-843-1751
Canaan Valley	Davis, WV	(304) 866-4121
Snowshoe	Marlinton, WV	(304) 572-1000
Whitetail	Mercersburg, PA	(717) 328-9400
Ski Liberty	Carrol Valley, PA	(717) 642-8282
Ski Roundtop	Lewisberry, PA	(717) 432-9631
Blue Knob	Claysburg, PA	(814) 239-5111
Hidden Valley	Somerset, PA	(814) 443-6454
Seven Springs	Somerset, PA	1-800-452-2223

Fat-Tire Vacations

Bicycle Touring Companies

There are literally dozens of off-road bicycling tour companies offering an incredible variety of guided tours for mountain bikers. On these pay-as-you-pedal, fat-tire vacations, you will have a chance to go places around the globe that only an expert can take you, and your experiences will be so much different than if seen through the window of a tour bus.

From Hut to Hut in the Colorado Rockies or Inn to Inn through Vermont's Green Mountains, there is a tour company for you. Whether you want hard-core singletrack during the day and camping at night, or you want scenic trails followed by a bottle of wine at night and a mint on each pillow, someone out there offers what you're looking for. The tours are well-organized and fully-supported with expert guides, bike mechanics, and "sag wagons," which carry food, gear, and tired bodies. Prices range from $100-$500 a weekend to more than $2000 for two-week-long trips to exotic lands such as New Zealand or Ireland. Each of these companies will gladly send you their free literature to wet your appetites with breathtaking photography and titillating stories of each incredible tour.

Selected Touring Companies

Elk River Touring Center	Slatyfork, WV	(304)572-3771
Vermont Bicycling Touring	Bristol, VT	800-245-3868
Backroads	Berkley, CA	800-BIKE-TRIP
Timberline Bicycle Tours	Denver, CO	(303)759-3804
Roads Less Traveled	Longmont, CO	(303)678-8750
Blackwater Bikes	Davis, WV	(304)259-5286
Bikeworks	Elkins, WV	800-427-7428
Bicycle Adventures	Olympia, WA	800-443-6060

Appendix

The Quintessential Off-Road Bicycle

Old road-bike seat

Vintage frame

Bar ends

Two water bottle cages

Brake levers

Freewheel

Tough knobby tread

Replacement derailleur (again)

Chainrings (teeth missing)

Scuffed clipless pedals

Forks
(no suspension system=brain slosh
on rocky descents)

Repair and Maintain

FIXING A FLAT

Tools You Will Need

- Two tire irons
- Pump (either a floor pump or a frame pump)
- *No screwdrivers!!!* (This can puncture the tube)

Removing the Wheel

The front wheel is easy. Simply open the quick release mechanism or undo the bolts with the proper sized wrench, then remove the wheel from the bike.

The rear wheel is a little more tricky. Before you loosen the wheel from the frame, shift the chain into the smallest gear on the freewheel (the cluster of gears in the back). Once you've done this, removing and installing the wheel, like the front, is much easier.

Removing the Tire

STEP ONE: Make sure all the air is out of the tire. Insert a tire iron under the bead of the tire and pry the tire over the lip of the rim. Be careful not to pinch the tube when you do this.

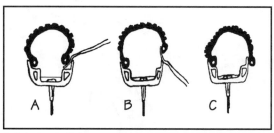

Pull the bead off the rim.

STEP TWO: Hold the first tire iron in place. With the second tire iron, repeat *step one* (three or four inches down the rim). Alternate tire irons, pulling the bead of the tire over the rim, section by section, until one side of the tire bead is completely off the rim.

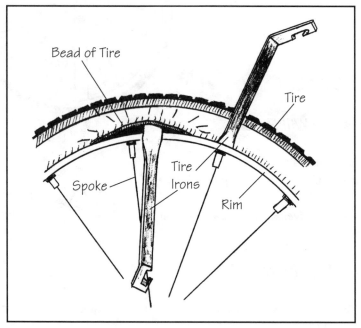

Using tire irons.

STEP THREE: Remove the rest of the tire and tube from the rim. This can be done by hand. It's easiest to remove the valve stem last. Once the tire is off the rim, pull the tube out of the tire.

Clean and Safety Check

STEP FOUR: Using a rag, wipe the inside of the tire to clean out any dirt, sand, glass, thorns, etc. These may cause the tube to puncture. The inside of a tire should feel smooth. Any pricks or bumps could mean that you have found the culprit responsible for your flat tire.

STEP FIVE: Wipe the rim clean, then check the rim strip, making sure it covers the spoke nipples properly on the inside of the rim. If a spoke is poking through the rim strip, it could cause a puncture.

STEP SIX: At this point, you can do one of two things: replace the punctured tube with a new one, or patch the hole. It's easiest to just replace the tube with a new tube when you're out on the trails. Roll up the old tube and take it home to repair later that night in front of the TV. Directions on patching a tube are usually included with the patch kit itself.

Installing the Tire and Tube
(This can be done entirely by hand)

STEP SEVEN: Inflate the new or repaired tube with enough air to give it shape, then tuck it back into the tire.

STEP EIGHT: To put the tire and tube back on the rim, begin by putting the valve in the valve hole. The valve must be straight. Then use your hands to push the beaded edge of the tire onto the rim all the way around so that one side of your tire is on the rim.

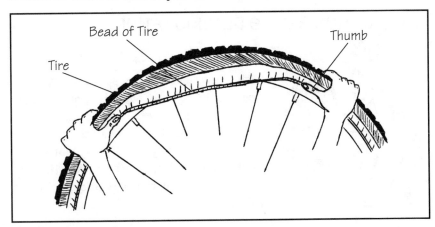

Tire   Bead of Tire   Thumb

Wrestling a tire onto a rim.

STEP NINE: Let most of the air out of the tube to allow room for the rest of the tire.

STEP TEN: Beginning opposite the valve, use your thumbs to push the other side of the tire onto the rim. Be careful not to pinch the tube in between the tire and the rim. The last few inches may be difficult, and you may need the tire iron to pry the tire onto the rim. If so, just be careful not to puncture the tube.

Before Inflating Completely

STEP ELEVEN: Check to make sure the tire is seated properly and that the tube is not caught between the tire and the rim. Do this by adding about 5 to 10 pounds of air, and watch closely that the tube does not bulge out of the tire.

STEP TWELVE: Once you're sure the tire and tube are properly seated, put the wheel back on the bike, then fill the tire with air. It's easier squeezing the wheel through the brake shoes if the tire is still flat.

STEP THIRTEEN: Now fill the tire with the proper amount of air, and check constantly to make sure the tube doesn't bulge from the rim. If the tube does appear to bulge out, release all the air as quickly as possible, or you could be in for a big bang.

When installing the rear wheel, place the chain back onto the smallest cog (furthest gear on the right), and pull the derailleur out of the way. Your wheel should slide right on.

LUBRICATION AVOIDS DETERIORATION

Lubrication is crucial to maintaining your bike. With a good lube-job, dry spots will be eliminated. Creaks, squeaks, grinding, and binding will be gone. The chain will run quietly, gears will shift smoothly, brakes will grip quicker, and your bike may last longer with fewer repairs. However, if you don't know where to put the lubrication, what good is it?

Things You Will Need

- One can of bicycle lubricant, found at any bike store.
- A clean rag (to wipe excess lubricant away).

What Gets Lubricated

- Front derailleur
- Rear derailleur
- Shift levers
- Front brake
- Rear brake
- Both brake levers
- Chain

Where To Lubricate

To make it easy, simply spray a little lubricant on all the pivot points of your bike. If you're using a squeeze bottle, use just a drop or two. Put a few drops on each point wherever metal moves against metal, for instance, at the center of the brake calipers. Then let the lube sink in.

Once you have applied the lubricant to the derailleurs, shift the gears a few times, working the derailleurs back and forth. This allows the lubricant to work itself into the tiny cracks and spaces it must occupy to do its job. Work the brakes a few times as well.

Lubing The Chain

Lubricating the chain should be done after the chain has been wiped clean of most road grime. Do this by spinning the pedals counterclockwise while gripping the chain with a clean rag. As you add the lubricant, be sure to get some in between each link. With an aerosol spray, just spray the chain while pedalling backwards (counterclockwise) until the chain is fully lubricated. Let the lubricant soak in for a few seconds before wiping the excess away. Chains will collect dirt much faster if they're loaded with too much lubrication.

Virginia Bicycle Clubs and Trail Groups

Ah, the folks you meet along the way...

IMBA (International Mountain Bike Association)
P.O. Box 412043
Los Angeles, CA 90041
(619) 387-2757

NORBA (National Off Road Bicycle Association)
1750 East Boulder Street
Colorado Springs, CO 80909
(719) 578-4581

Rails-To-Trails Conservancy
1400 16th Street, NW, Suite 300
Washington, D.C. 20036-2222
(202) 797-5400

League of American Wheelmen
190 West Ostend Street #120
Baltimore, MD 21230-3731
(410) 539-3399

Peninsula Bicycling Association
P.O. Box 5639
Parkview Station
Newport News, VA 23605
(804) 826-8313

Eastern Virginia Mountain Bike
Association
P.O. Box 7553
Hampton, VA 23666
(804) 722-4609

Hilton Cycling Club
9913 Warwick Blvd
Newport News, VA 23601

Tidewater Bicycle Association
P.O. Box 12254
Norfolk, VA 23502
(804) 588-1123

Tri-Power Cycling Club
1721 Laskin Road
Virginia Beach, VA 23454
(804) 491-1900

Williamsburg Bicycle Association
P.O. Box 713
Williamsburg, VA 23187
(804) 220-2879

Yorktown Bike Club
4521 Route 17
Grafton, VA 23691
(804) 898-6799

Richmond Area Bicycle Assn.
9013 Prestondale Ave.
Richmond, VA 23294
(804) 266-BIKE

Fredericksburg Cyclists
P.O. Box 7844
Fredericksburg, VA 22404

Charlottesville Bicycle Club
P.O. Box 475
Charlottesville, VA 22902
(804) 295-1212

Monticello Velo Club
19 Elliewood Ave
Charlottesville, VA 22903
(804) 977-1870

M.O.R.E. (Mid-Atlantic Off Road
Enthusiasts)
P.O. Box 1715
Centreville, VA 22020
(703) 502-0359

Potomac Pedalers Touring Club
P.O. Box 23601
Washington, D.C. 20026-3601
(202) 363-TOUR

Arlington County Bicycle Club
300 North Park Drive
Arlington, VA 22203-2599
(703) 751-8929

Reston Bicycle Club
P.O. Box 3389
Reston, VA 22090-1389
(703) 904-0900

Whole Wheel Velo Club
9514 Main Street
Fairfax, VA 22031-4031
(703) 323-0500

Winchester Wheelmen
P.O. Box 1695
Winchester, VA 22601
(703) 667-6703

New River Valley Bicycle Club
P.O. Box 488
Blacksburg, VA 24063
(703) 552-5563

Shenandoah Valley Bicycle Club
P.O. Box 1014
Harrisonburg, VA 22801

Virginia Tech Mountain Bike Club
meetings held in Squires, room 142
@ 8:00pm on Tuesdays

Blue Ridge Bicycle Club
P.O. Box 13383
Roanoke, VA 24033
(703) 344-6818

Central Virginia Bicycle Club
P.O. Box 1006
Lynchburg, VA 24505

Index

About the Author

When not conquering fiery new trails on his mountain bike or racing from town to town on his road bike, Scott Adams is hard at work writing his next guidebook, trying to play guitar, or learning the art of takeout. Adams, a native Virginian currently living in Richmond, is a freelance writer and author who lives his life to be outdoors. Nothing, he says, is more therapeutic than a long hike to the top of a mountain or an early-morning bike ride with no particular place to go. His other books include *Bike Rides from Beaver Stadium, Mountain Bike Madness in Central PA,* and *The Washington-Baltimore Mountain Book: Out of the Gridlock—Into the Woods.*

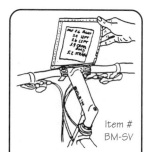
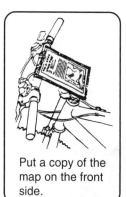
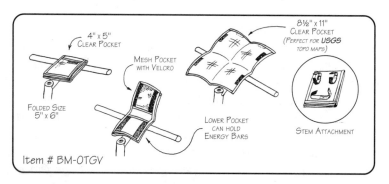

Other Books by Scott Adams

Mountain Bike Madness *in* Central PA
An Atlas of Central Pennsylvania's Greatest Mountain Bike Rides

From the southern tip of Rothrock State Park to the northern tier of Tiadaghton's Black Forest, *Mountain Bike Madness* takes you over rugged singletrack, through abandoned tunnels, across narrow train trestles, past magnificent vistas, and along Central Pennsylvania's most scenic mountain roads and trails. 18 rides highlighting the area's parks, natural areas, and scenery make *Mountain Bike Madness* the perfect guide to off-road adventures in Central Pennsylvania's magnificent backcountry.

Soft cover, 144 pages, 6 x 9
$10.95
ISBN 1-882997-02-6

Bike Rides from Beaver Stadium
An Atlas of Centre County's Greatest Bicycle Rides

For **Nittany Lion** Fans, each of the 24 rides in this unique guidebook conveniently leaves from **Penn State's Beaver Stadium**. Traveling in circuits of 5 miles to over 100 miles long, each ride leads cyclists of all ages and abilities along safe and comfortable roads, highlighting Central Pennsylvania's scenic beauty, historic landmarks, villages, towns, people, and food. Its unique hand-drawn maps, complete with barking dogs, stop signs, and cows, give this book a real sense of intimacy with the roads and the region. *Bike Rides from Beaver Stadium* is the perfect guide to bicycling in Centre County, Pennsylvania.

Soft cover, 128 pages, 6 x 9
$9.95
ISBN 1-882997-01-8

The Washington-Baltimore Mountain Bike Book
Out of the Gridlock—Into the Woods

An Atlas of the Washington-Baltimore Area's Greatest Off-Road Bicycle Rides.

Here is everything bicyclists need to know to enjoy off-road adventures in a region layered in more than its share of pavement. Plunge down steep, rugged singletrack into a quiet paradise deep within Catoctin forest, relax along leisurely lakeside trails minutes from the Beltway, and travel off-road through Virginia's scenic horse country, stopping only for a taste of wine from the region's great vineyards.

More than 100 specially designed maps illustrate 25 of the Washington-Baltimore area's greatest mountain bike rides, complete with historical tidbits, detailed directions, trail-maintenance hotlines, and more. This humorously illustrated atlas of off-road rides offers both novice and experienced cyclists the way out of gridlock and into the woods through the world's fastest growing sport.

Soft cover, 208 pages, 6 x 9
$11.95
ISBN 1-882997-03-4

Ask for these books at your local bookstore or outdoor store

—or—

order them directly from

Beachway Press
9201 Beachway Lane
Springfield, VA 22153-1441

include $2.00 shipping per item